ALL BUSINESS IS
SHOW BUSINESS

ALL BUSINESS IS
SHOW BUSINESS

SCOTT MCKAIN

Rutledge Hill Press®
Nashville, Tennessee

A Division of Thomas Nelson, Inc.
www.ThomasNelson.com

Published by Rutledge Hill Press, a Thomas Nelson company, P.O. Box 141000, Nashville, Tennessee 37214.

Library of Congress Cataloging-in-Publication Data

McKain, Scott.
 All business is show business / Scott McKain.
   p. cm.
 ISBN 1-55853-974-3
 1. Organizational effectiveness. 2. Consumer behavior. 3.Marketing—Psychological aspects. 4. Success. I. Title.
 HD58.9 .M435 2002
 659.2—dc21   2002001224

Printed in the United States of America

01 02 03 04 05 — 5 4 3 2 1

TABLE OF CONTENTS

CONTENTS

INTRODUCTION

Does it seem as though your customers are less loyal and more demanding? Do the people who buy your products and services now want it better, quicker, and cheaper—no matter how tough it is for you and your organization to deliver? At the same time, you may have noticed that your employees have changed. Perhaps you also feel your colleagues' work ethic is different than it used to be. How about you—and your professional standing? Could you benefit from a greater ability to "connect" with your customers and colleagues? Does your communication to them sometimes seem ignored or lost in the clutter?

If any—or all—of this sounds familiar, you are experiencing the impact of the cultural phenomenon this book will tackle: Today's culture relentlessly bombards us with entertainment.

The world we inhabit today is different from the one in which previous generations lived. Whether it is the latest television hit like *Survivor* or a classic movie we rent from Blockbuster . . . Howard Stern or Rush Limbaugh . . . Leno or Letterman . . . CNBC or ESPN—the entertainment industry surrounds us. My belief—based on twenty years of speeches and seminars to corporate America as well as building a $100 million business with my partners—is that show business has inundated us so thoroughly it has changed the way we buy and work. If you do not understand this fact and change the way you relate to customers and employees accordingly, you are going to fail, individually and organizationally.

Entertainment succeeds when it establishes an emotional connection with the audience. The more powerful the connection, the greater the success. You, too, must establish a passionate linkage with your clients and colleagues to create the type of loyal relationship that every business is seeking with its most important targets.

No matter what business you're in, it is show business. But let's get one thing straight: entertainment does not mean merely song and dance. As one friend asked, "Is my cardiologist in show business? I mean, I don't want him to tap dance his way to my bypass!" If that is what *you* are thinking, you need to broaden your view of entertainment.

Certainly, at times and in appropriate situations, entertainment's desired response is amusement. However, you would never think that a sense of light-hearted fun or slapstick mirth was the purpose of movies like *Schindler's List* or even *The Silence of the Lambs.*

The same emotional flexibility is true in business. For some organizations, creating and enhancing a connection with your customers and employees—your audience, if you will—will be found through increased humor and fun. Others, like a pharmacy for example, will establish their emotional bond through caring and concern by identifying with their customers and employees.

The purpose of this book is to examine this phenomenon and explain how you can make it work for you and your organization. We will also prescribe specific steps you and your business can take to sell and serve your customers, and manage and motivate your employees more productively in the twenty-first century.

It's SHOWTIME!

ONE

SETTING THE STAGE: YOUR BUSINESS IS SHOW BUSINESS

Not long ago, I experienced an incident that helped bring home to me the reality of today's marriage between entertainment and business. I returned to my hometown to present a lecture for an in-service meeting of the school's teachers and administrators. I have to admit that well before the program even started I was already feeling scared to death because sitting in the front row was one of my former elementary school teachers on whom I had a crush as a schoolboy.

I began my presentation with a very standard question that many speakers and authors ask to begin a lecture. "Let's start by having you tell me," I said, "what your biggest problem is. That way we will make certain we touch upon your most significant challenges."

I thought I knew the answers these teachers were going to give: student discipline, lack of parental involvement, changing curriculum, and lack of funding. Imagine my surprise then when my former teacher raised her hand and declared, "Scott, I believe education's biggest problem today is *Sesame Street*."

My response to her answer was immediate and profound: "Huh?"

My former educator asked me then, "Scott, who taught you your ABCs?"

"Well, my mother and my grandmother."

"Of course," she said. "However, for the last thirty years, young people have been taught their *ABCs* by Big Bird and Bert and Ernie. That means they arrive on the steps of this school for their very first day of formal instruction expecting to be entertained as they are educated."

My elementary school teacher was *still* teaching me.

For the past three decades and more, at the most basic level, we have taught everyone in this culture that education—as well as everything else that is supposed to happen in life—is going to be entertaining. Whether we approve of this phenomenon or not doesn't really matter. Either way, the fact remains that this is our world's reality. Entertainment is an integral part of our learning and training from an early age. So it behooves us to understand exactly what entertainment does.

As we've already said, entertainment doesn't just make us laugh. It is not just about "fun," and it is certainly not superficial. Instead, entertainment is about establishing and communicating an emotional connection with a designated audience. As I stated earlier: The more powerful the connection, the greater the success.

In the past few years, my business partner Tim Durham and I have had the opportunity to find out if this way of doing business really works. With practically no money to start our company—and thanks to Tim's brilliant vision and management—our first-year revenues totaled about $50 million. We are now a publicly traded company with revenues approaching $100 million, and all the companies we own are operating profitably. We have proven with Obsidian Enterprises that this approach can work. You, too, can use this approach even if you are in businesses like ours that aren't exactly considered glamorous—companies that build trailers or recycle tires.

The "ALL Business Is Show Business" philosophy is *not* about spending more money and blowing out your budget. It's not about dressing up in funny costumes and playing silly games. It's not even about "entertaining" your customer in the way that many organizations think (for instance, taking them to dinners and sporting events).

This philosophy *is* based on how you connect with the people who are most important to your business—your customers and colleagues. It's about understanding the need for high-touch solutions in a high-tech world. It's about realizing that relationships are more profitable than a mere sale.

> **"For the last thirty years, young people have been taught their *ABCs* by Big Bird and Bert and Ernie. That means they arrive on the steps of this school for their very first day of formal instruction expecting to be entertained as they are educated."**

RAISING THE BAR

The benchmark is rising in American business. A major new revolution is happening right now among customers and employees. Compare our current situation to what happened in the automobile business in the 1970s. Back then the Japanese car manufacturers revolutionized the automotive industry. Just about every study conducted at that time suggested that customers considered the Japanese product to be higher in quality than its American counterpart.

What happened next? Detroit went to work and re-engineered their cars to meet the new and higher customer demands. It did such a great job that customers came to say that American and foreign cars were approximately equal in terms of product quality.

At that point did the customer exclaim, "That's great! Just about every manufacturer now has a high quality product, so I won't ask for anything else"? Of course not. Instead, customers raised their level of expectations once again. Whether or not this is what automotive manufacturers wanted to happen is irrelevant. Their customers raised the benchmark for them. Customers next proclaimed, "I have a higher quality product. Now, I want better service!"

Service then became the name of the game in the automotive industry. This is when we started to see car dealers stay open later. (Some service bays even began to remain open until midnight!) I was fascinated when General Motors added roadside assistance to segments of their product line. If you run out of gas, and have a mobile phone, call them, and GM will bring gas to you. If you have a flat tire—even in your own driveway—they will come fix it! Not too many years ago it seemed that the only automotive manufacturers with a roadside assistance plan were Mercedes, Lexus, and Rolls Royce. Now you can get the same service on your GM car. This is clearly a revolution in the automotive business. Customer demands

> **The *ALL Business Is Show Business* philosophy is about understanding the need for high-touch solutions in a high-tech world. It's about realizing that relationships are more profitable than a mere sale.**

have successfully enhanced the level of service provided by the manufacturer and the dealership.

Is it reasonable to expect customers to stop raising their demands? Obviously, the answer is *no*. Are you willing to lower your demands when *you* are the customer?

Customers are assuming that you have a quality product and a modicum of good service; otherwise, you would probably have already fallen by the wayside. In today's world, these customers are taking product quality and service commitment for granted. Now, they are increasing their demands and raising the benchmark again. They are now saying: "Good is not good enough! If you want my business, amaze me! Knock me out! Make an emotional impression I won't forget." In other words, these customers, who were raised in a culture where they expected to be entertained as they were being educated, now expect to have an emotional connection as they are served, trained, and employed. The emotional bonding that we discussed earlier is the single most important element you can build into your professional relationships in today's marketplace. Unless you reorganize, redirect, and recast your efforts to attract this changing customer, your organization is nothing short of doomed.

In an issue of his *Trend Letter*, *Megatrends* author John Nesbitt said, "Want to sell, train, manage, motivate? First, you must entertain. In today's world of change, entertainment is now assumed to be an integral factor in everyday life." A recent article in the *Harvard Business Review* agrees: "The corporation is primarily a stage upon which you 'showcase' your bid for your customers, employees, and prospects."

The United States Chamber of Commerce, in its magazine *Nation's Business*, featured a cover story entitled "Entertailing." This new word is a combination of "entertainment" and "retailing." The essence of the article is that if you are not adding the factor of entertainment to your business, your organizational goose is beginning to cook. The article examines several businesses, especially a chain of music stores called MARS that have revolutionized the retail concept in the music

Customers are now saying, "Good is not good enough! If you want my business, amaze me! Knock me out! Make an emotional impression I won't forget."

industry through integrating entertainment into the experience of both employees and customers. By making MARS a fun place to be, musicians not only want to shop there—they want to work there as well! Loyal employees inspire customers to be loyal by providing an emotional connection that goes beyond mere products and services.

As I watched the luggage carousel spin around long after the last bag had been removed, I knew I was in trouble. A brokerage firm in Norfolk, Virginia, had asked me to speak to their high net worth clients. However, since the meeting was a Monday luncheon, I had traveled across the country in a pair of jeans and a sweatshirt. As I grasped the thought that my suitcase was nowhere to be found, I realized this was not the proper attire to address a meeting of multi-millionaires.

The woman at the airline baggage claim was cheery. "Don't worry," she told me, "we have another flight from Atlanta first thing tomorrow morning. Your bag will surely be on that flight." Equipping me with a small shaving kit of necessities, I departed for my hotel. The next morning, right on time, I was once again strategically stationed by the baggage carousel—and, once again, discovered that my luggage and I were taking separate vacations.

I was met with the same cheery response. "There's one more flight in an hour—it should be on that one." Keeping to myself the thought that the bag really *should* have been on the flight with me, I anxiously awaited the next flight from Atlanta. And, once again, I was disappointed.

Now, I was at a point of desperation. A room full of folks worth seven figures and more were going to convene in ninety minutes to hear me speak—and I needed a suit! Dashing to my rental car, the television commercial of Men's Wearhouse and their founder, George Zimmer, popped into my head. I called information from my cell phone and was connected with their downtown Norfolk store. A woman with a wonderfully pleasant voice answered—only to hear me immediately stammer that I needed help. "I have a speech in less than an hour and a half and my luggage has been lost. I need a suit, shirt, ties, shoes, underwear—everything! And I need to walk out of your store in an hour. Can you do it?"

Without hesitation, she immediately responded—just like the store's founder in his commercials—"Sir, I guarantee it!" *Wow!* Notice at this point, if Men's Wearhouse can do what she and the store's founder have claimed, they aren't merely excellent—they are amazing!

She said, "Sir, the only thing I need to know are your sizes—suit, shirt, shoes and so forth. We'll be ready." I gave her the requested information and sped to the store.

Sprinting in the front door, a well-dressed man standing next to a short woman said, "You must be Mr. McKain." Wiping the perspiration from my forehead with the sleeve of my sweatshirt, I smiled and asked, "What was your first clue?" I noticed he had two suits lying side-by-side, with shirts and ties strategically placed inside them. Both were great looking outfits.

"I didn't know if a navy suit or a charcoal suit would best compliment your current wardrobe, so I wanted to show you each in your size," he told me. The tiny woman next to him was introduced as the store's tailor. As soon as I could try things on, she would start altering the pants so that I could depart the store at the necessary time.

The service was nothing short of astonishing. I even bought an extra blazer that could go with the pants of my new charcoal suit in case the luggage remained missing an extra day. The suit, shirt, tie—even socks and shoes—were of the highest quality. In fact, I have to admit that I had never shopped Men's Wearhouse before because I assumed the clothes there were not of the style I could find, for example, at a Nordstrom. I was wrong. The materials and selection rivals any department store. However, the service at Men's Wearhouse makes an emotional connection that keeps customers coming back.

When I arrived on time for my speech, I smiled as I walked into the conference room because I received a couple of compliments on my suit. When it came time for my presentation, I began with the story of the local Men's Wearhouse.

Three points about why this is important to the "ALL Business is Show Business" philosophy that we will be discussing in this book:

Excellence isn't enough in today's business culture. I expect every store that sells men's clothes to have suits that will fit me, as well as a satisfying line of accessories. The amazing *experience* I received at Men's Wearhouse is what separated them from the pack of competitors in my view.

Amazed customers cannot wait to tell others about their experiences. I told several millionaires that very day. *And, I'm telling you right now!* This book will help you craft amazing experiences that will earn you the kind of "standing ovation" response I am giving Men's Wearhouse. There's no better way to build your business than have your customers help you.

Men's Wearhouse had never received any of my money prior to this experience because they had never connected with me on an emotional basis. It is important to note that *emotional connections always precede economic ones* in today's business culture. When they fulfilled my emotional needs—not merely my product requirements—they created not only a customer, but also a fan.

EFFICIENCY VS. EMOTIONAL PERSUASION

Ask yourself, "What is Nike's business?"

If you are from the old style of business thinking, you probably would say that Nike's business is the shoe business. But Nike understands that its business is not shoes—it is lifestyle.

Nike's fairly recent entry into the golf ball manufacturing business is an example. I would venture that most people who buy the Nike ball really aren't examining it with regards to whether it is a two-piece ball or wound; the materials of the core of the ball are interesting but not persuasive. Instead, you buy the Nike ball because you want to play like Tiger Woods; your emotional drive overtakes the product specifications. In today's marketplace, you can build the better mousetrap—or golf ball—and no one will care unless they are emotionally connected.

Other visionary organizations like Starbucks, Disney, and Microsoft understand this same realty. These organizations realize that a vast difference lies between being efficient and being persuasive.

An *efficient* advertisement that tells you factually what a movie is about does not move you to get up and go to the theater. A *persuasive* advertisement generates word-of-mouth, gets people talking about the product, and gets the seat of your pants into the seat of your local theater. It creates an emotional bonding between the movie (the product) and the audience (the customer). Show business understands that the only way to get you to spend money on a movie is to *persuade* you to go to the theatre and dole out your hard-earned cash.

The critical element in persuasion is the emotional connection between the persuader and the persuadee. Yet, what most organizations—and professionals—clearly lack is an understanding of the need for emotional connections in business, and the knowledge of how to create them.

I recently noticed in an issue of Delta Airlines' *Sky* magazine an article suggesting that more than 70 percent of companies believe that customer service has improved over the past five years. An equally high percentage of customers believe that service has declined. How can this be true?

My belief is that corporate America holds the conviction that *efficiency* is synonymous with *service*. One of my clients was bragging to me before a recent presentation about how much he had improved his service levels. His company was now answering the phone before the third ring and delivered product orders within forty-eight hours. He could not understand why customers were not becoming more loyal.

The problem is that customers are using a different measuring stick. Customers are blending the terms *service* with *emotional experience*. In other words, the vast differences in definitions are creating vastly different perceptions about service.

It is vital to emphasize, however, that "ALL Business is Show Business" is *not* about how to merely motivate customers or employees. If you constantly have to be conducting "rah-rah" sessions to fire up the troops, I am convinced either you are communicating the wrong message, or you have the wrong troops. This book is about how to engineer strategies and systems that will enable you to take the passion you and your people should already have and translate it in a manner that has greater effectiveness and is congruent with today's culture.

Many of today's top business thinkers and writers are preaching the importance of discipline in management and for organizations. I couldn't agree more. "ALL Business is Show Business" is a philosophy that takes this approach to the next level. In other words, I don't quarrel with much of what is being said in other leading business books. My experience in the trenches helping build a company, however, has taught me that it is important to have the right philosophy, and it is imperative that we find strategies so that we can transmit our viewpoint to customers and employees in a manner that is emotionally compelling.

SEEING BEHIND THE MASKS

At a recent convention where I was giving a speech, the CEO's presentation stressed his company's sales growth as it added business locations. Imagine my surprise when the Vice President of Marketing leaned over to me and whispered, "Growth covers a multitude of sins!" What a perfect comment!

When we are in an expanding economy, a business's growth can mask a massive amount of mistakes in how it deals with its customers. They might be taking their business elsewhere because it isn't performing as well as it should, but the business doesn't miss the disgruntled customers because new ones are there to replace them. This is why we often see a "shakeout" when the economy tightens. Companies that were taking customers for granted and not providing the kinds of emotional experiences required in today's culture—companies that were, in effect, growing only through expansion and acquisition—find themselves without loyal customers. The growing economy disguised the company's mistakes. Managers who fail to look beyond the numbers—and beyond the mask—are in for a disappointing surprise.

A shrinking economy can create a mask, as well. When the times get tighter, employees tend to stay in their current situations because they are fearful of making a change. Employers assume their business is staffed with loyal employees because turnover is low. When the inevitable upturn arrives, however, if the company hasn't provided a positive experience, the best people bolt for the door.

I actually had a sales manager tell me a while back that he didn't believe in spending much on training because, "These people are going to leave anyway." Would you want to work for someone like that? Me neither. The only people at that place running faster to get out the door than the employees are the customers. Shame on those managers who fail to look beyond the numbers and discover both customers' and employees' needs for emotional connections.

Please do not believe for a second that this book is about throwing away all of your established, yet persuasive, ways of doing business during this revolution we are discussing. But if your career—or your organization, department, or team—isn't as successful as you would like, you are not going to get there by working harder on your old plan. Think of the film *Hoosiers*. It was very old-fashioned, yet it was a huge hit. It took old ideas and made them fresh through the intense emotional connection the audience felt with the characters. You need a new way of thinking. Taking a fresh look through new eyes at old ideas can lead you to a smashing success. Look at some of your more established practices and ask yourself how they can be updated to enhance the emotional connections you are making with colleagues, customers, and prospects.

SHOW BUSINESS STRATEGIES

Show business—and the manner in which it maximizes the emotional connection with the audience to achieve maximum profitability—can help us understand the steps we should take to enhance our organizations. A five-step process will help us build and grow positive emotional experiences for our customers and employees:

1. Target the experience
2. Extend the experience
2. Repeat the experience
3. Upgrade the experience
4. Update the experience

TARGET THE EXPERIENCE

How does the product (in other words the film, the television show, the book, the play—or *your* product or service) play to its target audience? Have you precisely defined your prospective audience? (By the way, "anyone with a check that will clear" is not a precise enough definition!) If you do not know who your audience is, the chances are pretty good that you are not going to connect. Variety shows intended for a generic audience—like the *Ed Sullivan Show*—are basically a thing of the past. The entertainment companies now aim to target us with tight accuracy. ESPN does not worry too much about the viewing habits of homemakers. The Lifetime Channel isn't going to be concerned if football fans bypass it when they are zapping channels.

Imagine if you were putting on a play that is highly irreverent, erotic, and controversial—and then find that your audience is a group of clergy. Imagine Barney the dinosaur performing inside a maximum-security correctional facility. Obviously, these examples are absurd. However, they illustrate the point that if you do not know your audience, you cannot be a success. Evaluate your initial product and service—or management techniques—against the standard of how they meet the demands of the audience for whom you are seeking to "perform."

If, for example, you are a financial consultant, you gear the product to the needs of the prospect. It is vital to note that the product (just like a movie) must meet the emotional (not merely financial) needs of your customers and prospects to achieve success. That's why it is hard to sell retirement plans to young executives. Mortality hasn't sunk in yet. Of course, the other side of the coin is like the old joke about the life insurance salesperson that calls the ninety-year-old woman. She politely declines his request to purchase life insurance because, she tells him, "At my age, I don't even buy green bananas!" If you fail to precisely target your audience, you will never be able to develop a performance that will have the maximum emotional impact.

Do not base your product decisions exclusively on demographics. A zip code-based marketing program merely means you are targeting people who have chosen to spend a similar amount for their dwellings. It tells you very little about how they might *feel* about the products and services you offer. Take your research deeper.

EXTEND THE EXPERIENCE

This step explains why we saw so many *Jurassic Park* lunch boxes, notebooks, bedsheets, action figures, yo-yos, and more! One of the ways we need to emulate the show business model is by continually asking the question: "What are other additional products and services we can offer that will allow our audience to continue to purchase our experience?" The Nike approach we mentioned earlier is explained by this step as well. You see the familiar "swoosh" logo everywhere. By extending the experience, you give customers an opportunity to purchase additional ways to enjoy the emotional connection you offer.

However, the extension has to make sense. Several years ago, I had the chance to be an actor in a small German film called *Stroszek,* the story of German immigrants unable to adapt to life in the United States. I play the role of the banker that repossesses their mobile home. The movie ends when the main character commits suicide. And for some strange reason, unlike *Jurassic Park* or *Toy Story,* there were no *Stroszek* lunch boxes or bedsheets. Why? The answer is obvious: these were not extensions that "fit" the experience. There was, however, a very successful documentary released on the life of the director, Werner Herzog, that examined his wild passion for filmmaking. The documentary helped extend the experience of *Stroszek.*

The extension of the experience sometimes requires highly innovative thinking. But if the movie business can do it, so can yours!

REPEAT THE EXPERIENCE

The reason that *Titanic* has become the biggest box office hit of all time is because of the number of repeat customers it has secured. Even though the movie lasts well over three hours, people want to see the film again and again. In other words, not only do filmmakers look for additional ways for the audience to purchase the experience generated by the emotion of the movie through licensed products (the extension we discussed in the previous point), they also seek to develop a product that (in show business parlance) has "legs." A movie with legs is a film that has a longer than usual life at the box office. It is the kind of movie that attracts repeat business. It brings people in to see the movie not just once, but again and again. A list of the top hits in the history of film—from *Star Wars* to *E.T.*—clearly illustrates that the key to enormous profitability is found in obtaining repeat customers.

Isn't the same thing true in your business? The real key to earnings is the repeat customer. If you are an accountant, for example, the lifeblood of profitability is not found in a person for whom you prepare taxes once and never see again; it is in advising, consulting, and preparing taxes for the same clients year after year after year.

The success of a recent small movie illustrates the point. *Memento* is the story of a man trying to track down his wife's killer. That sounds pretty standard. The plot device that makes *Memento* remarkable is that the leading character has no short-term memory. The screenwriter/director of the film tells the story backward! The storyline starts at the end and works its way back to the beginning. This plot device leaves the audience as confused as the leading character. When you do get to the twist at the end—which, of course, is actually the beginning—the first thing you want to do is see the movie again, armed with all the information you now possess. *Memento* enjoyed the success it did because it is structured in a way that makes you want to repeat the experience.

Your organization also needs to create an experience that your customers and employees will want to repeat.

UPGRADE THE EXPERIENCE

Take notice of the many ancillary products now created by show business. From home video to pay-per-view, from the creation of

DVD to laser discs, studios are always seeking ways to persuade the customer to upgrade the purchase.

The difference between merchandising and upgrading is that merchandising persuades you to purchase additional items whereas upgrading persuades you to invest more in the initial product after you have already purchased it. In other words, the question the movie studio asks is, "Once I get you to buy a ticket to the movie, how do I find another way to get you to pay more for that same product?" How do I get you to take the purchase to a higher level?

Part of the answer for your business is to find new methods of delivery. Are there new ways that you can deliver your product or service to your customers so they will pay more even after they have made their initial purchase? Movie production companies have this down pat. They offer the original movie, and then they upgrade the video by offering the director's cut or scenes not found in the original. With DVD they can now provide even more upgrades like behind-the-scenes clips describing the making of the movie. Software companies are also masters of the upgrade. Once you have purchased something from Microsoft, you can be assured you are going to be contacted in a few months to buy an upgrade. This process seems to be repeated over and over again. It was enormously expensive for Microsoft to develop the code for a product like Power Point. Now, however, each sale creates increasing returns because the cost of the disks and packaging is so low. Add additional revenues to Microsoft from product upgrades, and you find that Power Point becomes more valuable—instead of diminishing—the longer it is in the marketplace.

This strategy has created a new area of thought in economics. While the law of diminishing returns has been taught as a primary principle in understanding business finance, leading economists (primarily at the Santa Fe Institute in Santa Fe, New Mexico) are now discussing the law of increasing returns.

UPDATE THE EXPERIENCE

An *upgrade* is taking the current product purchased to a higher level. It is seeing *Lethal Weapon* and then buying the DVD. An *update* is seeing *Lethal Weapon 2 , 3,* and *4.* If they make *Forrest Gump 2,* I am going to be in the theatre. I want to see what happens next to good old Forrest. I want an update on what is happening in his life.

As we mentioned earlier, repeat business is the key. Part of the reason that mysteries—the classic whodunits from Agatha Christie novels to the O.J. Simpson case—have fascinated us is that we all want to see what happens next. If your customers are emotionally connected, they will be looking forward to an update.

One of the great showbiz practitioners of this philosophy is Madonna. Few people would say that Madonna is a great singer. However, even fewer would dispute that she is a fascinating entertainer. By constantly remaking herself—by creating a sequel of her own image—she keeps us interested in what she will do next.

A UNIVERSAL APPROACH

You might think these show business strategies apply only in the area of mass-market retailing. But nothing could be further from the truth. Because we have all—customers and employees alike—been socialized for three decades by entertainment, all businesses have been impacted.

The old cliché in Hollywood is that they don't call entertainment production "show art." They call it "show *business!*" The same principles that apply to the entertainment industry also apply to my line of business—and yours. The Retail Marketing Institute recently released a study conducted by the America's Group research firm headed by marketing virtuoso Britt Beamer. The amazing finding produced by this analysis was, in essence, that more than 70 percent of customers would tend to go someplace else to make a purchase if it was more entertaining to do business elsewhere.

Does that statistic shock you? You may be asking, "What about those products we have worked so hard to engineer? What about those employees we have spent millions to train? What about all of the things I learned in business school or management training that were supposed to make a difference to the customer?" It's time to update your perspective.

Your customers and employees are not looking for a floorshow. Inserting the entertainment factor into your products and services—and making your business a show business—is not about balloons and costumed characters. It is not mere hypocritical frivolity. We should be serious about our products and services. But more organizations need to understand they should not be so grim about themselves or their image. If a movie fails to make an emotional connection with the viewer, all the technical expertise in the world will accomplish little. And the same is true with every other business in the world today.

This philosophy works with employees as powerfully as it does with customers. Recent studies suggest that 74 percent of employees

> **More than 70 percent of customers would tend to go someplace else to make a purchase if it was more "entertaining" to do business elsewhere.**

say they would quit where they are currently working and take a position with another organization for comparable pay if it were more fun to work elsewhere. Remember, though, when people use the word *fun*, they're not talking simply about games and giggles. They're looking for the emotional connection they found with Big Bird and Oscar the Grouch—on a professional level. They don't want just a job—they want a relationship.

Forming a good relationship with your employees is even more important when you consider the trend of hiring freelancers. Take *Titanic* as an example. Director James Cameron, who headed up the production of this $200 million effort, is not technically an "employee" of the studios that put up the money! The cinematographers he hired, the scenic designers who constructed the elaborate set of the great ship, even the actors and extras, are all independent contractors rather than employees.

If you look at recent issues of leading business magazines like *Fast Company*, you will find indications of a similar trend in the world of industry. These articles suggest that we all work, in essence, for ourselves; we are "free agents." All a company does is "rent" their employees' time, talent, services, and abilities. In the past, these "employee services" were traditionally "rented" by the employee to only one company. The "free agent" concept hypothesizes that in the future we will be renting our services to multiple employers for varying lengths of time. This is a structure the movie business has been applying for many years. It is a great example of how a business of the future will be managed, funded, and administered. But the only way any business can ensure it will be able to get the best free agents is to provide experiences these independent contractors want to repeat—emotional connections they desire to continue and enhance.

Mark Cuban, owner of the NBA's Dallas Mavericks, understands this point completely. He outfits his locker room with more amenities for his players than any other in the league. When criticized for providing multi-million dollar superstars with more pampering than they deserve, his response, in effect, was, "Who wouldn't want to work someplace where you are treated like that? No matter how much money you are paid, you want to know the organization cares for you as something more than a mere employee." As the world of all businesses becomes more like a movie or the NBA, your business is going to have to employ similar strategies to ensure your success in attracting the best free-agent talent.

No matter what your organization does, no matter what your distribution channels are, no matter what services you offer or what

The bottom line is that your customers and employees are going to have an emotional experience because of their contact with your organization, whether you like it or not. Your responsibility—and challenge—is to provide them with the kind of emotional connection that will inspire loyalty.

products you manufacture, no matter whether you are a CEO or a new sales representative, your business is show business. The "ALL Business Is Show Business" philosophy will work for your business (and your personal life). And quite frankly, you don't have a choice. The bottom line is that your customers and employees are going to have an emotional experience because of their contact with your organization, whether you like it or not. Your responsibility—and challenge—is to provide them with the kind of emotional connection that will inspire loyalty.

Entertainment is an approach that can be translated into *your* business. I would suggest that just as you couldn't imagine running a business without keeping accurate financial records, we are at the point now in our culture where you shouldn't be able to conceive of managing an organization without utilizing the principles of entertainment. That is what this book is about—helping your business establish a powerful, successful, emotional connection with your customers and employees.

ALL BUSINESS IS SHOW BUSINESS QUIZ

On a sheet of paper, write the words *emotional connections* at the top. Under that make two columns: *organization* and *your name.* Make a list of the emotions your company provokes in its customers and prospects. Next, make a list of the emotions *you* stimulate in your customers and colleagues.

If you cannot think of any emotions that you or your organization arouses, then you have a lot of work to do! If you are able to list several emotions on each side, you must next ask yourself, "Are these the *appropriate* emotions to create customers for life and energized, loyal colleagues?"

- How does your product or service fit specifically into the wants, needs, and desires of your audience? In what ways do you "miss the boat"?

- What additional avenues are you providing for your customers to buy into your "experience"?

- What do you do to encourage your audience to repeat the experience of doing business with you? (A mere thank-you card is not nearly enough.)

- How are you set up to upgrade the initial product? How do you allow a person to spend more money on your product?

- What is the sequel? How do you show customers what happens next? How interested are *your* customers in your next move?

Two

THE CHANGING IMPACT OF TIME AND EMOTIONS

Are you old enough to remember the popular sixties song, "The Times They Are A-Changing"? The man who wrote the song is now in his sixties. Along the way, America continued to change—and people, including Bob Dylan, did too.

Culture has made some dramatic shifts, and these changes have had a remarkable impact on people—how we buy and work. In this chapter we will look at how culture has changed and the implications this change has on our behavior in our business:

- How customer and employee behavior has been transformed.

- How emotion—in addition to economics—is driving today's business.

- How to build amazing experiences through product, service, and experience.

- How successful organizations create emotionally satisfying experiences.

HOW CUSTOMER AND EMPLOYEE BEHAVIOR
HAS BEEN TRANSFORMED

What are some of the main changes in customer and employee behavior? For one thing, people value their time more. They are more demanding in terms of *what* they want, and they have higher expectations for product and service performance; in other words, they focus on *how* after they have selected the *what*. People today have different standards about consumer and employee loyalty than previous generations. And last of all, they focus on feelings as much as product technology and service delivery.

Do you recall what it was like to go to the drive-in restaurant? It was always a big deal for my family. I would be in the back seat with my sister, while my mother and father were in the front seat. Dad would pull into a parking space at Cliff's Drive-In and—believe it or not—park! He would roll down the window and place our order. (Restaurant speaker technology hasn't greatly advanced through the years.) About five minutes later, here would come the waitress. Her tray was piled high with food; she was chomping on chewing gum; sometimes she would even be on roller skates.

Dad would roll the driver's side window up a couple of inches so the tray would fit on the glass. Food would be dispensed, arguments about who had the most French fries would be resolved—and then a strange thing would happen. Everyone inside the car would look at one another before the meal began and there would always be an instant where children and adults alike thought, *Wow! We're eating in the car.* In those days, eating in the car was forbidden. It was something you absolutely did not do—unless you were visiting the drive-in.

Times have changed. Now we do not drive in; we zip in and out of drive-thrus, and if more than three cars are ahead of us, we're frustrated and impatient. Eventually, with our burgers balanced on our laps, we head back into traffic.

Do you remember when we had to go to the bank on Friday afternoons to get enough money to make it through the weekend? Long lines would snake through neighborhood financial institutions as people prepared for their weekends. And the only way you could do your banking was through a teller. Banks probably thought they had reached the ultimate in customer convenience when drive-thru windows were installed, but today we do not stand in line for the teller or wait in the drive-thru. Instead, we zap our card through an ATM. ATMs started out as equipment available only at banks. Now, as you know, they are a phenomenon found everywhere. From gas stations to hotel lobbies, from airports to casinos, wherever you go, you do not have to wait for cash, because an ATM is there. ATMs have become such a part of the national landscape, we do not even think about how we will acquire cash anymore. I am ashamed to admit it, but many times I have boarded an airplane to travel across the country and realized I only have five bucks in my wallet. It really does not worry me to leave home for a couple of weeks with only five dollars in my pocket because I know I will be able to get cash anywhere, anytime from an ATM. A friend of mine has commented on how he can do his banking (at the ATM), drop off his dry cleaning (in the all-night slot), and take care of business at the post office (at the stamp machine or 24-hour window) on his way to the office—all by 6 A.M.!

The times have certainly changed. The old "back fence" over which gossip and other information were exchanged is a thing of the past. Now, the Internet and e-mail has become the gossip and bad joke conduit of our times. E-mail has increased the convenience and speed of communication, and thus the speed of business. It reminds me of the television commercial in which a young employee gets on an elevator in his corporate headquarters on the first floor. As the elevator ascends, stopping on several floors, the people getting on the elevator congratulate him on the memo. At the end of the commercial, the chairman on the top floor wants to see our young e-mail hero. While this television spot is obviously spoofing the speed at which business is conducted today, it nonetheless makes the point that there is no time to wait for information.

When we stop to look, we see change everywhere. People have changed as well. The technological changes that have driven the speed of transactions have impacted the buying behaviors of customers and the performance of employees. People have been transformed because their expectations have altered.

Previously, businesses could improve upon their ability to deliver on these altered expectations by simply being more efficient. That is, in part, why the drive-in became the drive-thru. But that strategy is just not going to work anymore. Can you promote yourself as the most efficient stockbroker now that I can make a trade on any one of several Internet sites just as quickly as you can? When I have the same access as you do to the markets, there is not only the phenomenon of disintermediation, there is also, more importantly, a transformation of my expectations of value and what I'm willing to pay for.

Exposure to the media is another way in which our society has changed. Nielsen Media Research recently released a study that indicates the average American television set is on around eight hours per day! You are probably saying to yourself, "Well, *I* don't watch that much television." That is not the point. The point is that your customers and employees *do*. No matter how good your organization is at selling and serving, no matter what your proficiency is in training and motivating, you are not going to be able to overcome the training that people in this country are receiving from their extensive television habits. This may not be the ideal situation. In business, however, we

Previously, businesses could improve upon their ability to deliver on altered expectations by simply being more efficient. That is, in part, why the drive-in became the drive-thru. But that strategy is just not going to work anymore.

must deal with situations the way they *are*, rather than the way they *should be*.

For years we have heard business speakers cite the buggy whip story. This cliché focuses on the assumption that the last company to make buggy whips probably manufactured the best buggy whips you could imagine. The problem was, as the story goes, people did not need buggy whips anymore after the automobile was invented. The product had become irrelevant because mechanization transformed the entire culture.

The current shift in culture is much more subtle than the move into mechanization. That is why so many companies fail to understand why their business must become *show business*. They clearly understand technology has changed. They just do not seem to take that knowledge to the next logical conclusion. Not only have products and services changed, expectations of the people who buy those products and services have been radically transformed.

In today's channel-zapping, faxing, FedExing, e-mailing, instant-response world, there is a new currency—time. Today's stressed-out consumers and employees value this new currency as much as money. This means that as people's expectations and values have changed so has the impact of your product or service. Now people value your product or service not only based on economics but also on their ability to save time and create emotional connections. To develop the *show business* business, you must reevaluate what your organization is all about. You must ask yourself how your organization is factoring emotion and time into your delivery system.

HOW EMOTION IS DRIVING TODAY'S BUSINESS

In the September 5, 2001 edition of *The Wall Street Journal*, a front-page article tells the story of a restaurant analyst for a brokerage firm in Little Rock who is having great success in picking the right stocks for her clients. What's the secret to Lynne Collier's success? If customers are willing to wait in line for an extended period of time to enjoy not just the food but the experience of the restaurant, it is one in which she wants her clients to invest. P. F. Chang's, The Cheesecake Factory, and Outback Steakhouse are examples of restaurants she caught on the upswing. Seeing the decline in the waiting lines at other restaurants helped her get her clients out of stock positions before their corporate shares declined.

Why would any organization be arrogant enough to assume that the same people we have just discussed—the ones driving through restaurants, getting their cash from ATM machines, and zapping channels on a daily basis—would want to *wait* for anything? There is only one reason: an emotional experience worth waiting for and savoring.

The traditional focus of business strategy has always revolved around economic principles—costs, growing market share, enhancing shareholder value. A significant portion of the focus of our business strategy must shift to emotional principles.

This is the single factor today's consumers—and employees—value more than time.

Emotional involvement is a very real part of the value of the relationship an organization has with a customer or an employee. The traditional focus of business strategy has always revolved around *economic* principles—costs, growing market share, enhancing shareholder value. I believe, however, given the cultural and behavioral changes in customers and employees we have previously discussed, that a significant portion of the focus of our business strategy must shift to *emotional* principles.

We have already learned that customers want (some would say need) an emotional contact and relationship with an organization to remain loyal to its products and services. Those 70-plus percent of customers we talked about earlier who would change where they do business if there were a higher entertainment factor someplace else are customers who are obviously not feeling a strong connection where they are already doing business. The missing element is neither product nor price—it is emotion.

The key to the box office success of all the Walt Disney animated classics is that people see the movies over and over again. They saw them as children—and then they take their children and feel the emotional connection anew. That also helps to explain why sports fans are so loyal. Even when their team loses a game they attend, the emotional connection with their favorite team drives them to repeat the experience.

For several years in the McKain household a Monday night ritual took place. My wife Sheri and her sister Leslie watched the television program *Melrose Place* together. Sheri happens to live in California, while Leslie lives in Florida, but they would call each other during the commercial breaks and talk about what had just happened on the show. They wanted to share the program's emotional experience with one another.

One of my best friends, Mark Mayfield, a noted speaker and humorist, and I do the same thing during sporting events. During televised golf tournaments, we will call each other and say, "Can you believe that shot?" Even though we live over fifteen hundred miles apart, we have shared many sporting events because of our emotional connection to the games.

Have you ever seen a film where you just had to go to a coffee shop afterward to talk about it? Why? Even though we appreciated the product of the filmmaker and the service of the theater, we still must connect and share the experience. That is another advantage of creating a customer experience that is amazing and astounding—*customers are driven to share their experiences.*

Why do we hang on to a stock long after we should have sold

with the hope that it just might come back? Is it economics? I would suggest it is emotion. Why do we go back to the dry cleaner who puts the crease in the wrong place but greets us cheerfully by our first name? Is it because the dry cleaner is cheapest—or because we feel an emotional connection? When we need the services of a funeral home, do we sit down and comparison shop for the best value for our dollar—or do we go to the establishment whose demonstration of genuine compassion touches our hearts?

Don't get me wrong: I am not saying that economic realities can be ignored. But the predominant way we have defined business is causing us to miss what is now happening in the marketplace. If you disregard emotion and define business as being solely about economics, you will fail in today's culture. If you ignore the emotion, the economics won't work.

Show business elicits an emotional response from the audience. A comedy seeks the response of laughter and fun. A drama may want to make you feel melancholy, angry, or motivated. In other words, strategies for show business demonstrate what organizations should be planning today—how to elicit the desired emotional response from the intended audience. You may or may not have planned what your customer's experience will be, but either way that experience will inevitably take place. A bland experience for the customer will elicit no response, loyalty, or word-of-mouth marketing. A negative customer experience develops a strong negative emotional response. Customers cannot wait to repeat the negative experience—except they will relive it in front of their friends, instead of at your business. They will make certain through their negative testimonial marketing that everyone they know will hear about what a lousy time they have had doing business with you. However, a highly positive customer experience generates loyal customers, repeat business, and marketing of the highest value. Happy customers tell friends so they can repeat

The purpose of any business is to profitably create emotional connections that are so satisfying to customers and employees that loyalty is assured.

the experience together. Friends want other friends to have positive experiences, so they will recommend your business.

All this stems from the fact that as times change, people change. Entertainment has changed our culture, and therefore, people have changed. If you and your organization do not . . . you won't be in business much longer.

In today's world of change, you cannot succeed by merely working harder on the old plan. You and your organization may need a new plan. Management guru Peter Drucker is often attributed to saying, "the purpose of business is to obtain and retain customers profitably." Obviously, if any organization obtains customers—in other words develops products, services, and practices that are executed by employees in such a way as to attract customers—and then retains those customers in a profitable manner, that business will be a success. In fact, in a recent interview, Drucker said, "the *only* function of a business is to create customer value and innovate."

Consider a new way of thinking about the purpose of business: The purpose of any business is to profitably create emotional connections that are so satisfying to customers and employees that loyalty is assured.

All businesses are going to have to learn to make powerful emotional connections in the future if they want to survive. I believe that in just a few short years, we will not even be talking about customer service. Customer service will seem as old-fashioned and outdated as yesterday's buggy whips. What visionary businesses will be trying to create rather than customer service is a fabulous *customer experience*. People want to repeat pleasurable experiences, and they want to avoid repeating disappointing ones. I am not merely reciting the old sales training line about selling the sizzle with the steak. I am telling you that in these times of change, the sizzle *is* the steak!

It is amazing to me how some senior executives—who scoff at the notion that emotion drives business—become extremely passionate when they talk about *their* customer experiences. When they are viewing their own business, they become highly product oriented and analytical. When they play the role of customer, they become emotional just like everyone else.

I was discussing this point recently with a top executive at one of the nation's largest technology-driven companies. He was disagreeing with the concept of "ALL Business Is Show Business"; he said the focus must be kept on economics and technology. However, he commented on how he wanted to continue to share information with me and perhaps bring me to lecture to his organization. As he talked, he pulled a product I recognized out of his coat pocket, a "pocket briefcase" from Levenger's, a mail-order catalog house and retail outlet that specializes in "tools for serious readers."

I am a Levenger's fanatic. I have become hooked on buying fountain pens and all kinds of accessories from them—including the pocket briefcase. I noted to the executive, "Oh, I see you shop at Levenger's too."

His entire demeanor changed. His eyes rolled back into his head, his knees buckled, and his body swayed. "Oh man!" he exclaimed. "Are they the best or what? When I receive their catalog, I just want to call up and say, 'Send me one of everything.'"

I told him I had the same feeling. I also told him how impressed I was with many things about their operation—the knowledgeable way their operators take orders over the phone, they way they can customize the nib of the pen to fit the style of your writing specifications, the quick manner in which orders are filled, and the wide variety of useful products that they sell.

His head bobbed up and down in enthusiastic agreement. "I just can't get enough of Levenger's."

After he made this last comment, I couldn't resist asking a question. "What if your customers felt the same way about your company?"

A long silence followed. "Oh, that could never happen in our business," he stated.

"Why not?" I asked.

"Because customers just cannot feel that way about our type of business."

"Why not?" I asked again.

After much thought, the look on his face changed, and he smiled. "I see what you're saying." He realized he had assumed customers could not feel that way about his product because of *his* focus on the technology—the hard assets—of what his company manufactured. It had never before occurred to him that customers could get emotional over the same product he approached from an analytical perspective.

Peter Drucker, in an interview with the business magazine *Business 2.0* in October 2001, said, "I can say that no financial man will ever understand business because financial people think a company makes money. They think money is real; that it is the end result."

What if your customers felt about you the way you have just read that two customers feel about Levenger's?

HOW TO BUILD AMAZING EXPERIENCES

Building an amazing experience today will require "thinking outside the box." What you did in the past was quite possibly exactly the right approach for those circumstances. The situation has changed— and so have your customers. Now it is time to start anew to build an experience based on today's rules, one that amazes today's customers. You will need to focus your strategies in three areas:

1. Product
2. Service
3. Experience

PRODUCT

Amazing customer experiences start with an amazing product. How does your product go beyond merely pleasing the customer into creating an experience the customer finds breathtaking? Customers expect quality to be designed into your product, so let's be clear: If you focus on emotion to the exclusion of product design and quality, you misunderstand what I am saying. Customers see through a false façade pretty quickly. The emotional experience needs to be firmly based on product quality.

Let me give you an example. On my desk right now is a product I love—my little Canon ELPH camera. It is so tiny; it easily fits in my briefcase when I travel. It turns on with a single touch of a button that is easy to find. It is compact, yet it has a flash, zoom, and built-in settings so I just have to point and shoot. And the film can only be inserted one way—the right way—making it idiot-proof for

Building an amazing customer experience requires "thinking outside the box." The situation has changed—and so have our customers. Start anew to build an experience based on today's rules, one that amazes today's customers.

the photographically challenged (like me). This little product amazes me because I don't have to make any sacrifices. Previously, I had to sacrifice portability in order to have all the features I wanted. Or I had to sacrifice the features I wanted to have portability. I love this camera—and I have an emotional connection with it, because it provides the vehicle (pictures) I use to relive emotional events. It is proof that product design can inspire emotional connections.

The little icon of the smiling face that greets you when you turn on a Macintosh computer is another good example. For your computer to smile at you is a very small thing—yet it is one that for millions of Macintosh users is part of an emotional bonding. The product and the emotional link are intrinsically joined.

The design of many products is troubling at best. Dr. Ken

Dychtwald, author of the best-selling book *Age Wave*, was the first person I heard outline how absurd some product design is for an aging marketplace of Baby Boomers. For example, I was staying at a hotel recently and wanted to receive a fax in my room. When I tried to give the number to my client, I couldn't find it. The problem wasn't that the number had been left off the phone but that some under-thirty graphic designer with perfect eyesight had no idea how difficult it would be for a forty-six-year-old hotel guest to read such small type. And I guarantee you many more professionals in their mid-forties stay at that hotel than graphics designers in their mid-twenties. Apparently, no one who will be using the product—in this case the hotel telephone—was ever asked if there were ways to design the product to make it more functional and, thus, more emotionally appealing.

A product can also be so technically amazing that it is difficult for the customer to use. This may again contribute to a less than positive emotional experience. For instance, people who really "know" the Internet give me incredible grief that I have an account with AOL. "That's for kids," they chastise me. And they're right: America Online *is* for kids—and grandparents and parents and people like me. To a great degree, AOL is dominant because it is a product designed to make what is daunting to many people—the Internet—so easy to use.

On the other hand, a product cannot be so sloppily engineered that customers notice a lack of product quality as part of their customer experience. In that case, no matter how satisfactory the service or experience, the product destroys any chance of a relationship. For example, it didn't matter how low the price was on that small car from Yugoslavia—the Yugo. And the cute, feel-good advertising campaign had no lasting success. The car was of such an inferior quality that very few people were willing to take advantage of the low cost; the product was so lacking that no one cared how cute it was.

SERVICE

As you plan the creation of an amazing customer experience, the manner in which you serve your changing customer is obviously a part of the equation. The talk of the future will center around customer experiences—rather than customer service—I don't mean to imply that service would become passé. Instead, I am suggesting that customers are blending all parts of their experiences into a meaningful whole.

Service, unfortunately, has been thought of as something separate from the product. Most organizations with whom I have worked over the last two decades completely separate those responsible for the product from those responsible for the customer service. That's insane!

When you attend a movie, the product (the movie) may be wonderful, but if the theater is dirty, if the popcorn at the concession stand is stale, if the bulb on the projector is so old that the movie isn't as bright as it should be—well, you get the idea—you aren't going to be satisfied. The product might be magnificently assembled, but if the service is not there, the customer is not going to want to repeat the experience. Customer service is an important piece of the equation for any customer—even those who maintain that they are "price buyers."

It is difficult for some of us to think about moving to the realm of experience in business when we find that most customer service in this country stinks. I'm tired of being put on hold, I am sick of voice mail jail and being told to "check the Web site for answers." I refuse to go into restaurants with signs that state "The Customer is Number One" over tables that haven't been cleared while you watch employees smoking outside. I'm done doing business at places where employees won't help you because you are asking for something "out of their department." I'm ready to scream at telephone customer service representatives who would rather pass me off to a supervisor to tell my story once again than help me on the spot.

It took a long time for businesses to get used to the notion that customer service was every bit as much a part of the customer's decision-making process as the product. Many companies still do not get it. They may *say* they do—but customers know better.

In Wal-Mart's initial days their goal was to be the number one supplier for those customers who considered themselves "price buyers." Under the guidance of the late Sam Walton, extensive research was done to determine exactly what segment of the marketplace considered themselves to be "price buyers." According to the story, the number was only 17 percent! After finding this statistic, the Walton family realized that if Wal-Mart stores were not clean, well lit, fully stocked, and staffed with courteous employees, even the 17 percent "price buyers" would go someplace else. That is why Wal-Mart has greeters at the front of every store. They let you see from the moment you walk in the door that Wal-Mart is still in the business of service, as well as "low prices everyday."

An emotional experience without quality service eventually equals displeasure or anger. Quality service without an emotional experience eventually equals boredom. Quality service plus emotional experience equals emotional connections. Service must be engineered into the customer experience.

EXPERIENCE

A great product and great service will cause a business to obtain and retain customers and employees. A great emotional experience will cause a business to connect with its customers and employees, to bond with them and secure a lifetime of loyalty. Creating such a bond is one of the hardest parts of the relationship.

The reason that thinking about the customer experience is so challenging is because it takes customer service—the nontechnical, and often more difficult, aspect of business—to a much higher level. Most professionals feel more comfortable dealing with the concrete, definable, and measurable aspects of business. We are so proud of the technical aspects of the products we sell—mainly because we have spent so much time trying to develop a superior product—that we think like manufacturers and marketers rather than customers and prospects.

At a meeting recently where I was the keynote speaker, Ric Duques, Chairman and CEO of First Data Corporation, was discussing the speed of electronic transactions with the customers of First Data's well-known division, Western Union. First Data's mission is basically to enable consumers and businesses to safely and securely pay anyone, anywhere, anytime. First Data serves nearly 2.6 million merchant locations, 1,400 card issuers, and millions of consumers—instantly! If you facilitate the speed at which transactions take place, you assist in creating more transactions.

Duques made clear during the meeting that, while transactional speed is the mechanics of the business, it is the *relationship* with the customers of all First Data's divisions that is the future of the business. "If we don't enhance the value of our relationships," he told me, "they won't value our ability to process transactions." In other words, Duques realizes you can spend literally billions of dollars to create the most amazing technology, and then spend millions to train employees to provide service that is efficient, but you will never maximize your investment until you create emotional connections with your customers. These connections are based upon experiences with your organization.

Customers are blending the *facts* about the quality of your product and the delivery of your service with the *feelings* they have about the experience of doing business with you. Customers often do not distinguish between fact and feeling. If they feel something strongly enough, the rationalization factor kicks in. In other words, they will

When customers connect with your product, they are interested. When customers connect with your service, they are appreciative. When customers connect with your experience, they are amazed; they want to repeat the experience you provide; they become loyal to the product.

rationalize with "facts" (that may or may not be true) to justify the way they feel. As the entertainment culture dominates our society, this effect will become more pronounced. That is why I stated earlier that I believe in a few years customer service, in and of itself, will become antiquated. Let's continue to use a show business phenomenon from a few years ago as an example. Why was *Titanic* so successful? It reached the level of success it did because director James Cameron followed the three steps we have discussed in this chapter.

First, the product is phenomenal. It is of the highest caliber. The technical aspect of this film is without peer. The special effects are absolutely amazing. The performances from the cast are superb. The screenplay is well written.

Second, the service of the film reached the same high standards as the product. In the early days of the film's release, the producers demanded that *Titanic* be shown in only the best theaters—the ones with the most sophisticated sound, projection, seating, and so forth. The producers wanted to make certain that the service provided the customer was part of what was engineered into the product. They knew you can make a grand film, but if you show it on a small screen with bad sound, you are not serving your customer. Third, it is in the area of experience that *Titanic* really excelled. This is the key to why it moved from being merely a successful film—a movie that was well made, well acted, and well displayed—into the biggest box-office hit of all time. The genius of James Cameron in this film is his clear understanding that it takes more than special effects to capture the heart of the audience. It takes an amazing story and rich character development to make the audience feel connected. People will go to see the same movie over and over again if they feel a connection—an experience—that moves them emotionally. The love story that drives the film and the characters we come to know create an emotional experience that makes this movie a classic.

When I read about the mass of people who died on the actual *Titanic*, I understand that fact intellectually. When it is portrayed through a compelling love story, I connect with the incident emotionally. A similar situation exists with the Civil War. I can read about the scores of fatalities at the Battle of Vicksburg and memorize the statistics. Yet when I read the story of just one soldier trying to make it back home in the brilliant novel *Cold Mountain* by Charles Frasier, I have a powerful emotional experience I will never forget.

When customers connect with your product, they are interested. When customers connect with your service, they are appreciative. When customers connect with your experience, they are amazed; they want to repeat the experience you provide; they become loyal to the product. Customers want to repeat experiences that positively impact them in an emotional manner.

HOW SUCCESSFUL ORGANIZATIONS CREATE EMOTIONALLY SATISFYING EXPERIENCES

What companies make you starry-eyed? Is it the service from Nordstrom? Maybe it is the gadgets at Sharper Image? Perhaps it is the wonderful SUV you drive from Cadillac? Examine your purchases of the past year or so. Which ones have made you swoon?

Let's use the grocery business as an example of creating emotionally satisfying experiences. I grew up in a family that owned a "mom and pop" grocery store in our small town. To our family, the product of our store was the groceries that people purchased. Women (at that time they were the usual customers) would come into the store with their grocery lists, fill their shopping cart, and take the products home to prepare for the evening meal. It was part of a weekly ritual.

However, for today's customer the game has dramatically changed. As we stated earlier, the most important currency for customers now is time. One study quoted at a recent meeting of the National Advisory Group of Convenience Stores and Petroleum Marketers stated that only about 38 percent of grocery store purchases are food to be cooked and consumed at home. That is a surprising statistic.

One of the greatest examples of an organization changing to keep pace with how people have changed is found at Marsh Supermarkets in Indianapolis. When I go into a local Marsh grocery store, I find the normal selection of food items. But inside the neighborhood Marsh, I will also discover a travel department, dry cleaners, shoe repair shop, bank, upscale cigar store, gourmet coffee bar, sushi bar complete with a chef, a video store with my favorite movies, a full-line pharmacy, a total cosmetics salon, a wine selection that rivals the best in town, and a nursery complete with closed circuit television so you can monitor what your child is doing while you shop.

By the way, what if you do not have time to shop? No problem. You can pull into Marsh, drop off your grocery list, return later, and pick up your groceries already bagged and billed to your credit card. Or, if you prefer, for a very small charge, you can fax or e-mail your grocery list to Marsh, and they will deliver the groceries to your door. If you only want milk and bread, you will find it in the front (not the back) of the store. The old philosophy in the grocery business used to be: Put it in the back so customers will have to walk by other stuff they might buy. Marsh now is saying: Some customers want to get in and get out—let's put these essentials up front to help them. On the other hand, if you only need bread, milk, and gas, Marsh also owns a chain of convenience stores. In fact, you'll find a Village Pantry convenience store in the parking lot of the large Marsh supermarket near my former home. Why? If your need is a gallon of milk and a tank of gas, you can do that in the parking lot. Marsh understands that customers have changed and the important currency is time.

Don Marsh, CEO of Marsh Supermarkets, told me his company dramatically changed the game they were playing when they realized their competition was not other supermarkets. Rather, Marsh views McDonald's and other convenience and time-oriented businesses as their main competitors. The dual-income household has to decide how they could get the greatest number of errands completed in the least amount of time. "We wanted to make certain we were able to provide that convenience for our customers," he told me. Clearly, he also realized that if it was quicker and less of a hassle to drive-thru at a restaurant and then hit separate stores—the dry cleaners and bank, for example—customers would not be visiting the Marsh Supermarket.

At the same time, however, some of the large food warehouse-type stores that promoted the lowest prices in Indianapolis are either encountering economic hard times or closing completely. Why? Does this mean that consumers have changed so dramatically they are no longer interested in price? No, if the prices go too far apart, customers will still change where they make their purchases. However, the old, tired, and irrelevant adage that consumers are solely price sensitive, especially in substandard economic times, does not hold water in today's culture where time and experience dictate loyalty.

OBSIDIAN ENTERPRISES

Tim Durham, one of the two men to whom I dedicated this book, came to me a few years ago with a unique proposition. He said, "Scott, I believe it when you say that 'ALL Business Is Show Business.' Let's take very mature and unglamorous businesses and prove that the concept works. I'll own a sizable majority of the company and run the day-to-day operations. Your job is to integrate the 'ALL Business Is Show Business' philosophy into our organization and management. Keep an eye on things, and remind us when we get too 'corporate' for our own good. We will change the way these organizations deal with customers and employees since we know they have changed with the culture."

Of course, Tim had many more ideas to implement than just my philosophy. One of the things he believes is that many entrepreneurs do not have exit strategies. In other words, some guy uses his welding skills out in his backyard to make a trailer to haul equipment. Then, someone else asks him to make another one. He is asked for another, then another, and all of a sudden he finds himself in the trailer business. The problem for this entrepreneur (as it is for most) is that he is not a businessperson; he is a *trailer* person! As his business grows, he often is faced with three problems:

First, product quality alone is not sufficient. It might have sold the first several trailers, but now he needs customer relationships and emotional bonding—something he is not usually equipped to create.

Second, the entrepreneur is often not an expert in the manufacturing processes necessary to achieve maximum efficiencies. As his customers were moving to the "just in time" ordering philosophy, his company finds itself having difficulty satisfying the demands of the customer.

Third, the more successful the business, the less likely the children of the owner are to want to follow in his footsteps. The family's new affluence from their success means that now the children want to be, as the Willie Nelson/Waylon Jennings song says, "doctors and lawyers and such." They do *not* want to get their hands dirty in a low-tech, highly physical business. This means that our entrepreneur now finds himself with a more successful business than he might have imagined a few years earlier . . . and nothing to do with it after he retires.

Tim's idea was that we could buy these businesses at a reasonable price and employ the elements of the "ALL Business Is Show Business" philosophy to the operational side—and his expertise in manufacturing on the production side. We would develop strategies in these specific companies that would enhance the emotional connections with their clients (meaning more sales) and employees (meaning higher productivity). Because we were increasing revenue from improved sales and lower costs, the value of our company would grow. We could then leverage the enhanced value we had created in our acquisition to buy more companies and repeat the process. We could bring a more sophisticated management strategy to these businesses because of our experience and create enhanced customer relationships, while keeping entrepreneurs excited by maintaining their involvement in the original businesses.

The results have been nothing short of phenomenal. We're getting a return on our initial—and very small—investment that is astronomical. Obsidian Enterprises efforts have made me a millionaire—

> **Have you and your organization changed to meet the needs of your customers and employees?**

and Tim Durham a multi-multi-millionaire. And, it all starts with understanding today's customers, potential customers, and colleagues better than the competition does—and appreciating them in a manner that is almost always overlooked by today's managers, sales professionals, and organizations.

Later in this book, I'll tell more of the story of how Tim Durham and his colleagues executed these concepts to turn our small investment into a $100 million publicly traded company in a short period of time. By using Tim's expertise and the "ALL Business Is Show Business" philosophy all of our acquisitions achieved immediate and remarkable growth in mature markets. Because the culture and people change and these changes impact personal behavior businesses have to change also. From restaurants to grocery stores, from banks to television, we have all observed dramatic and amazing organizational change. What is often overlooked is that these changes have not only influenced the culture, they have transformed the behavior of customers and employees, as well.

So, if you acknowledge and understand these behavioral changes in your customers and employees, you must ask yourself this question: Have you and your organization changed to meet the needs of your customers and employees?

Remember the old Far Side cartoon called "What We Say to Dogs and What They Hear"? In this cartoon were two panels of equal size. The one on the left was what we might say to our dog. In the drawing, the guy is saying things like, "You are a bad dog, Rusty! You have to keep out of the garbage, Rusty! I'm telling you for the last time, Rusty!" The other panel is what the dog hears. The drawing is identical, except the caption is: "Blah, blah, blah, Rusty! Blah, blah, blah, Rusty! Blah, blah, blah, Rusty!"

I think that is how we often feel in business. We put together a wonderful mission statement or prepare an expensive annual report; we coordinate PR efforts, and we post notices on bulletin boards. And then, after all this work, we often get the feeling we might as well be standing on the street corner going, "Blah, blah, blah."

Now that you realize *your* business is show business—and we have explored how customers have changed—we find that an important question remains: How do you communicate your message to customers and employees during these entertainment-focused times?

Once again, show business has the answer. Each of the next three chapters will provide one of the three keys to preparing your organization (and you) for success in the next decade. These three keys are:

1. *Develop a high concept:* The short, powerful statement that really defines your business identity.

2. *Tell a Powerful Story:* Building a compelling story that springs from the high concept and creates an emotional connection with your customers and colleagues.

3. *Create the Ultimate Customer Experience (UCE):* Developing the definitive experience for your customers (and employees) by exemplifying everything that is compelling about your story and putting it into "action" for those who are most important to your business.

You can think of this like the process of producing a movie for your audience. The high concept is the short, powerful phrase that defines what your business (movie) is about. After you define a high concept, now you begin to write the story (screenplay) of your organization. When you finish the story, it is time to put all the elements together to produce the UCE (emotional connection). It's where your organizational production hits the stage for your customers.

In the next three chapters, we'll look at each of these key strategies—and you'll begin to understand how to apply them to your personal life and your business.

ALL BUSINESS IS SHOW BUSINESS QUIZ

- List the ways you feel television has impacted our society in terms of customer behavior. For example, are people more skeptical now because of the media? Are they more demanding now because they are exposed to more options?

- Analyze the ways you have changed your business and/or product to relate to these changes.

- How have you made it quicker for customers to do business with you? Do you value your customers' and employees' time when responding to their needs?

- What new plans do you have to speed up customer and employee response, while at the same time enhancing the relationships you have with customers and employees?

- Adjusting to the world in which we live is not about working harder. It is not even about working smarter. It is about working *different*. Remember, in today's world of change you cannot succeed by working harder on the old plan. What are some elements of your new plan?

- When was the last time you picked up your phone and called your company to see what happens to *your* customers? If people would recognize your voice, have someone else do it and listen in. You may be surprised. If you are not providing easy telephone access for your customers, how in the world are you ever going to emotionally connect in a positive manner? The answer is obvious: You can't.

◦

THREE

THE "HIGH CONCEPT" CONCEPT

See if you know what movie goes with each of these three phrases:

- "Bomb on a bus!"

- "Shark attacks!"

- "A small group of soldiers find a family's lone surviving son and escorts him back from World War II."

If you knew any—and you probably knew all—of these movies, you have just proven that the "high concept" concept works. The concept of a movie, book, or play describes in great detail what the plot is all about. It is an involved description of the work of the author, director, playwright, or screenwriter. However, because we live in channel-zapping, fast-paced times, people will not listen to a long, involved concept. Therefore, Hollywood grabs the customer's attention by using a minimum number of powerful words—a high concept.

Some current business books, most notably *The Attention Economy* by Thomas H. Davenport and John C. Beck, propose that attention is the most valuable commodity in all of business today. I appreciate Davenport and Beck's point, but I would qualify their position. The three-step process of show business—developing a high concept, telling a powerful story, and creating the ultimate customer experience—will mean you are not only able to attract attention, but you are also able to gain loyalty from customers and colleagues once you have it. Attention that doesn't create loyalty is, in most cases, detrimental to the organization. Attention is important, and it is certainly the first step; however, I would suggest that customer loyalty is actually the most rare and valuable commodity in business today. However, we can't take that second step to customer loyalty if we haven't made the first step. We need to use a high concept to grab customers' attention—and keep it!

Mind share always precedes *market share*. You won't receive a percentage of customers' purses unless you obtain a percentage of their minds. In today's culture, that means you need to break through all the clutter out there and plant your message above the confusion. People have no time to listen and learn, consider and contemplate. So how do we grab their attention? You do it with a short, powerful, attention-grabbing phrase that identifies your uniqueness while involving your audience in a memorable way—a high concept.

When I started to understand why high concept was so important to Hollywood, I also learned how important it could be to all businesses. Having a high concept has meant literally hundreds of thousands of dollars to my company. Using it for our businesses with Obsidian Enterprises has enhanced our ability to grow quickly to more than $100 million in annual sales. My clients—like Conseco Capital Management and their mutual fund division under the guidance of Senior Vice President Bruce Johnston—practice it every day and have found it to be one of the most important factors in helping them succeed in the highly competitive marketplace of financial services.

My literary agent, Mel Berger of the William Morris Agency, successfully used a high concept to help focus the goals for the fundraising drive at his daughter's school. My e-mail inbox is filled with

> *Mind share* always precedes *market share.* You won't receive a percentage of customers' purses unless you obtain a percentage of their minds.

testimonials from organizations and individuals who have put the high concept into use and found that it:

- Focused their business.

- Identified weaknesses in organizations and departments.

- Enhanced communication with customers and employees.

- Stimulated referrals.

- Streamlined meetings.

- And, most important, made them more profitable and productive.

If you do not have an organizational and individual high concept, you are at a vast disadvantage to those businesses that have learned to phrase their messages so that today's changing customers and employees remember and connect with them.

When I mentioned "bomb on a bus," you undoubtedly thought of the movie *Speed*. Even though it took about two hours to watch the movie, the high concept allows you to explain the plot in a mere three seconds. That is powerful communication! The high concept can even be as short as one word. The mere mention of the word *shark* evokes the movie *Jaws*. The phrase "rescuing a family's lone son from war" is, of course, the high concept of one of the most powerful movies of recent times, *Saving Private Ryan*.

Visionary companies in today's show-business times understand that this same principle works for their organizations as well. Federal Express functions are based on its high concept "Absolutely, positively overnight." Even though corporate decisions may involve millions of dollars or thousands of employees, the most important question some one at FedEx can ask is, "How does this help us deliver a package from one customer to another 'absolutely, positively overnight'?" In a similar way, Domino's revolutionized the pizza business with its simple high concept: "Your pizza in thirty minutes." The use of these high concepts caught the attention of customers.

Visionary companies understand that customers or employees, who spend most of their time zapping through channels and driving through restaurants, are not going to have time to listen to a long, drawn-out explanation of what any organization does. People like this have a remote control in their heads. If you go on too long about your organization, you will get mentally "zapped" as they move their attention on to another "channel." In today's media-centered world, customers and employees with their short attention spans no longer stay focused for long, involved explanations.

WHAT MAKES A GREAT HIGH CONCEPT

You may be thinking that a high concept is the same as a mission statement. Mission statements, however, are internal functions that ensure everyone within the organization is "singing from the same sheet." They try to include a little something for everyone. Although

The high concept is a short, powerful, attention-grabbing phrase that identifies your uniqueness while it interests and involves your audience in a memorable way.

promoting diversity within your organization may be important, for example, very few customers will buy your product simply because of your position on this issue. Mission statements are absolutely worthless as a mode of customer communication. Customers do not have an emotional response to your mission statement. Customers do not care about your mission statement.

What makes a great high concept, whether personal or organizational? When we examine the elements of successful high concepts, we find they have most (if not all) of the six following characteristics:

1. Short

2. Powerful

3. Attention-grabbing

4. Interesting enough to generate audience involvement

5. Descriptive of your uniqueness

6. Memorable

KEEP IT SHORT

For some reason, in business we have been trained to believe the longer the answer the more important it must be. When someone asks about our company, we tend to think that the more detailed our answer is about what our company does, the more important and prestigious it makes our organization sound. In fact, exactly the opposite is true. When the explanation is longer, people tune it out. When it is short and powerful—a high concept—they respond. A high concept *must* be brief and to the point.

During the newscasts about the destruction of the World Trade Center, the story had many aspects. However, most news organizations led with a banner that said something like, "America Under Attack." Despite the vast amount of information that could be used to explain the story's myriad aspects, that really said it all. In fact,

Good high concepts have six characteristics. They are: (1) Short, (2) Powerful, (3) Attention-grabbing, (4) Interesting enough to generate audience involvement, (5) Descriptive of what makes you unique, (6) Memorable

the brevity of the high concept really encouraged us to acquire more information: Who was attacking us? How were we going to respond to the attack? Why was this done to America? All of these questions were generated in our minds by that one short, simple statement.

Your statement must also be brief in order to break through the clutter of information bombarding your listener.

BE POWERFUL

Successful high concepts use powerful words. FedEx's *absolutely, positively* leaves no wiggle room and, therefore, creates a powerful image. Power is also driven by the assembly of words that may seem incongruous, such as Southwest Airlines' high concept, which might be expressed simply as "Cheap. Safe. Fun." Nike saying "Just Do It" is one of the ultimate power statements and highly appropriate for the competitive world of athletics. "ALL Business Is Show Business" is much more powerful than "Many Businesses Are Show Business" because of its all-encompassing nature. Don't use bland terms like "improved" or "great customer service" because they aren't powerful and so many can make the same claim. For instance, you might say that Hallmark makes greeting cards, but in your heart you know what they really make is something you should send "when you care enough to send the very best." That's powerful!

GRAB THEIR ATTENTION

High concepts that rivet our attention have infinite value for the organizations that design them. During his reign as head of NBC, the late programming guru Brandon Tartikoff had an idea for a program perfect for the times. With the advent of MTV, nothing was on the networks that grabbed the nation's attention like the new cable upstart.

Television legend has it that when Tartikoff called producer/director Michael Mann to his office, he gave him an index card with a two-word, attention-grabbing high concept on it: "MTV Cops." This high concept inspired and described one of the biggest television hits of the eighties: *Miami Vice*.

Something new grabs our attention. Something that guarantees timeliness also grabs us.

INTEREST AND INVOLVE YOUR AUDIENCE

Your high concept has to be something that interests your potential audience and relates to their concerns. When I attend trade shows of various associations, I find high concepts about items I wouldn't buy—yet they are of vast interest to their intended audience. When I made a presentation at a State Association of County Governments recently, there was quite a commotion at a particular booth touting the high concept "What's old is new again." It was a demonstration for a new type of liner to help preserve sewer pipes. Wow! Yet, for those commissioners and officials, it was highly interesting information. Know your audience; then craft a high concept that will pique their interest.

Audience involvement should also be accomplished through the high concept. The audience will be involved whenever a statement makes them ask themselves, "What does that mean?" or, "How do they do that?" or, "What do they suggest I do next?" When customers or employees have dialogues with you—even inner dialogues—they are engaged and involved.

IDENTIFY YOUR UNIQUENESS

Following a presentation to a group of beginning financial consultants with Merrill Lynch, one of the attendees asked me to review this high concept statement he had prepared: "I will help secure your financial future."

My response: "Boring!" Every single financial consultant in America could say the same thing. As we discussed the importance of differentiation, he told me he was an Air Force pilot before becoming a financial consultant. I told him *that* was something that could make him unique. His high concept now is: "I'll fly you through financial turbulence." He recently sent me an e-mail to say his business has grown about 40 percent in the past twelve months.

His experience has taught me two important points about using a high concept that identifies your uniqueness:

First, when you develop a high concept, you make it possible for prospects who cannot remember your name to find a way to contact you. When someone calls the Merrill Lynch office and asks for the guy who can "fly me through financial turbulence," the receptionist knows whom they are requesting.

Second, when you develop a high concept, you are writing your own referral script. While we might want our clients to tell all their friends about everything our product or service can do for them, the real world does not work that way. With all the need for referrals in today's highly competitive marketplace, the high concept can be a tremendous marketing tool.

Think about how most of us were taught to ask for referrals: "Jim, have you valued the service I've been providing you and your family?" (Here is where you pray that the client nods.) "Great. Could I get the names of your forty-eight closest friends and relatives who also might be interested in my service?"

That's ridiculous! People in the real world do not talk like people in training classes or sales books. They will, however, casually share your high concept with someone as a part of normal conversation. Friends will use a high concept, like "Hey, call this guy. He's flying me through all the financial turbulence." A great test for your high concept is how it sounds when you slip it into regular conversation. Find a way to communicate what makes you uniquely you; make it a part of your daily interactions, and others will pass it on.

I mentioned earlier that one of the benefits of developing a high concept is that it can uncover weaknesses in organizations and departments. You may already be discovering a part of that as you read this chapter. If you are saying to yourself nothing really makes your organization unique, then you *really* have a problem. Companies that haven't differentiated themselves from their competition are grooming themselves for failure in today's changing marketplace. If you cannot describe how you are unique and worthy of business, your customers and employees can't either. If they don't know what makes you deserving of their business, why should they give you any?

One of the important principles in the show business industry is that you want to be derivative—but *different*. What this means is that all successful forms of show business derive from an inspiration that was probably generated elsewhere. Part of the key to understanding the art of successful show business is to tap into emotions and feelings that have already been established—while putting a unique spin on your product so that the audience believes it is being offered a new experience.

Old Navy stores are a good example of the success this strategy brings. A lot of clothing stores sell the basics—T-shirts, jeans, and so forth—but Old Navy's unique approach has made it successful. Old Navy started, believe it or not, as the warehouse stores of the Gap.

The executives at Gap, Inc. realized that to be more successful, they needed to differentiate the Gap Warehouse from the Gap—and Old Navy was born. The high concept was: "A whole new shopping experience with fashionable clothing and accessories for value-conscious customers." You will note when you visit Old Navy that several differentiating points create their "whole new shopping experience"—from the way the products are packaged and merchandised to the cordless headsets worn by employees. The reason for the headsets, as stated on the Old Navy web site, is a high concept in itself: "Make the job easier and look cool."

Gap executives first correctly defined their problem—Gap Warehouse stores weren't unique enough in the marketplace to be as successful as they desired. They may not have used this book's terminology, but they faced the problem we are discussing: What was the high concept of Gap Warehouse stores? By its very definition, a business like that would have problems developing a high concept that identified the store's uniqueness. ("Same stuff you wouldn't buy at the Gap, so we have it here at a discount." Not a great high concept.) Once the problem was identified the high concept—"whole new shopping experience"—could easily be created.

> **If you cannot describe how you are unique and worthy of business, your customers and employees can't either! If they don't know what makes you deserving of their business, why should they give you any?**

What makes *you* different? Sometimes your uniqueness will have nothing to do with your product! McDonald's corporate high concept—"You Deserve a Break Today"—does not talk about food. Take time to identify what makes you or your product special.

If you are having difficulty creating a basic high concept for your business, you are probably unfocused as a company, trying to be all things to all customers, fighting price battles without really knowing why and operating without a clear vision of where you are trying to go—thereby diminishing your effectiveness in the marketplace with both employees and customers. Use the high concept principle to focus and center your organization. Once you identify what makes you one of a kind, you will also identify many of your problems.

BE MEMORABLE

There is no telling what will make a high concept memorable. Some just are. Why do some great television shows or great musicians fail to find a large audience? That's part of why *all* business is show business. Just as in entertainment, a significant aspect of artistry is involved in the process of success. For instance, I am not certain what the ingredients are of a deluxe soft taco at Taco Bell. Does it have onions? I don't know. I *do* know, however, that a Big Mac is "two all-beef patties, special sauce, lettuce, cheese, pickles, onions, on a sesame seed bun." And none of us has forgotten an old lady saying, "Where's the beef?" Incorporate the other dimensions of a good high concept that we have talked about here, and you'll have a shot at being memorable.

A PERSONAL HIGH CONCEPT

The idea of developing a high concept is not just for organizations but for individuals, too. We *each* need a powerful, interesting, and individual high concept statement that clearly describes what it is we do. When someone asks the question, "What do you do?" most of us respond with a litany of our responsibilities. "What do I do? Well, let me tell you. . . I blah, blah, blah. . ." If we look closely, we'll see the listener's eyes glaze over. One of the most important aspects of the high concept is that it allows you to do for yourself and your business exactly what an excellent high concept does for a movie: *break through the clutter.* If an executive who loves golf receives a call from someone who identifies himself *not* as a financial consultant but rather as someone who will "help you raise your net worth and lower your handicap," my guess is that he or she will probably take that call.

You need to work on a dual track here. Organizationally, use these principles with your colleagues to develop a company or department high concept. Individually, use the high concept idea to develop a fresh way of presenting to others what you do. A lot of PGA professionals can hit the ball a long way. But when John Daly states that he's going to "grip it and rip it," we crowd around the tee box.

A personal high concept may affect your outlook as much as it does your audience's. After a speech to a huge audience at the American Payroll Association, I received a wonderful e-mail from a woman who had developed the high concept for her payroll department. What she was most excited about, however, was the renewed vigor she had for her job because of her personal high concept. Instead of being the "manager for corporate payroll," she now "deposits the money that finances the hopes and dreams of 10,000 people around the world." That may seem small to you, but it was *huge* to her. When you merely process checks, you are part of an emotionless system. When you make certain that 10,000 families can finance their lives, hopes, and dreams, you have added the power of emotion to your work.

DEVELOPING YOUR HIGH CONCEPT

We have defined a high concept, shown why it is a significant part of show business communication, and explained why it is so vitally important that your organization develop such a statement. Now comes the most important part. Now it is time for you to focus on how to develop *your* organizational and individual high concept statement. If all you do is read about this—and fail to actually develop a high concept—then all you have done is to "think outside the box" rather than "*do* outside the box." Didn't we mention a great high concept earlier? "Just Do It."

Keep the six points to a high concept in front of you. Remember, your high concept should be:

Short

Powerful

Attention-grabbing

Interesting enough to generate audience involvement

Descriptive of your uniqueness

Memorable

As I said earlier, you may not be able to achieve all six with your statement. For example, I don't think the Old Navy high concept is particularly memorable. It did, however, succeed in interesting the audience, identifying uniqueness, and making a reasonably short and powerful statement about the business. Four out of six isn't bad—in fact, it became a huge success!

Let's outline a few of the basic steps you can use. In this way, you will be able to create and craft a statement that will grab the attention of your customers, prospects, and employees, and interest them in what you and your organization is all about.

STEP #1

Start by examining your mission statement. You may be surprised I am suggesting this, since earlier I stated that customers do not respond to your mission statement. The reason they do not respond to your mission statement, however, is *not* because the information contained in the statement is inaccurate. It is ignored simply because of the *manner* in which the mission statement is presented. Within your mission statement are probably some very important ideas, values, and concepts about your organization. Your job is to "mine the gold" out of the statement.

Search through your mission statement for the points that make your organization superior to your competitors. This is the first step in determining what makes your organization unique. Also, look for the typical corporate clichés that cause your audience to "tune out." These phrases tend to talk about corporate niceties like "commitment to customers and employees." While it is certainly important for any organization to have these qualities, obviously *no* organization is going to say they are taking an opposite viewpoint! What organization could possibly say they are *not* committed to customers? Because comments of this type are so bland and generic, they fail to grab anyone's attention. A high concept attracts me to do business with your organization, in part, because I assume everything else is in place. Your customers are making the same assumptions, as are your employees. Remember, the goal here is to continue to streamline and refine the mission statement until it is condensed into a powerful high concept statement.

STEP #2

The second step in developing a high concept is to brainstorm with colleagues about the key words that describe your organization. During this brainstorming process, it is important to follow a specific pattern.

FREE ASSOCIATION

Get your group to shout out words that describe the organization. Naturally, some of these will be humorous. Complaints about the organization, the fact the organization "stinks," or others will undoubtedly be cited. This is an important part of the process. People think more creatively when they are thinking humorously. Do not try to shut off the "fun valve" here. The laughter will open the gates of insight. Also, do not evaluate the ideas at this point. You are looking for *quantity* not quality.

EVALUATE WORDS

Now that you have developed a "laundry list" of concepts about your organization, begin an evaluation phase. Ask the individuals in your group to select the ten words that have the most impact on customers and employees—as well as the ten that most accurately describe your organization and its strengths. After the members of your group have individually made their selections, have them pair up and share their selections with someone else in the group. They should then, as a team, develop a list of ten. Then, pair up the pairs of people—in other words, create groups of four for your next discussions. Have these groups develop a list of only five concepts. Notice what you are doing here is prioritizing the most important concepts, while at the same time ensuring that everyone in the process is being heard.

CREATE A PHRASE

After these groups have completed their work, take these five words from each group, put them on a flip chart or overhead, and begin discussion. Some groups will be surprised at what other groups believe to be important. Try to narrow down these words to the two or three most powerful, dynamic aspects and qualities of your organization. Then, create and craft a phrase that incorporates the concepts you have deemed most significant into your high concept statement.

CUSTOMER INTERACTION

Select a group of your customers (and, in some cases, *former* customers) and have them proceed through the same process. Look at the disparities in the concepts that have been chosen. You may find it fascinating that the qualities that are thought to be most powerful internally are *not* the ones your customers suggest. This is vitally important information if you hope to craft a high concept statement that has meaning to your potential customers. This should be an interactive and fun process for your customers or former customers.

ADVERTISING CAMPAIGNS NOT REQUIRED

By now you will have noticed that high concept statements are sometimes the advertising slogans of organizations. "Absolutely, positively overnight" has become part of the national lexicon. Yet some high concepts are not advertising slogans or time-saving guarantees. The Southwest Airlines' "Cheap. Safe. Fun." is not something they advertise. Instead, it is something they exemplify by how they execute what they do.

If you do not have access to the funds for an expensive advertising campaign, that shouldn't stop you from creating a high concept. The process of formulating a high concept is just as essential for a mom-and-pop business as it is for mega-corporations. In fact, a small, family-owned men's clothing store where I purchase clothes has succeeded with a simple high concept: "Since 1919: Timely Fashions—Timeless Service." A downtown variety store in a small South Dakota town battled new competition from a Wal-Mart with an effective high concept: "ANYONE can sell EVERYTHING. We KNOW you and what you need."

Your personal high concept will be the keystone of what you believe and what you advocate. For me, obviously, my high concept is "ALL

Business Is Show Business." Robert Schuller's is brilliant: "Tough Times Never Last, But Tough People Do." Olympic champion and motivational speaker Bob Richards had one that gave me chills because he communicated it so powerfully: "There Is Genius in the Average Person." The high concept of the New Testament is found in the verse John 3:16: "God loved the world so much that he gave us his only Son."

Creating a high concept statement is one of the most valuable communication tools you and your organization can develop during these changing, "show business" times. Don't forget that if you need ideas and inspiration on these statements, merely go to the television page of any newspaper and see how succinctly classic films and shows are described in short high concept statements. I guarantee that if they can describe a $200 million movie in seven to ten words, you can do the same for your organization.

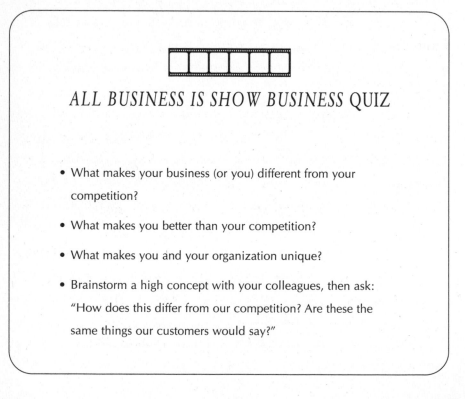

ALL BUSINESS IS SHOW BUSINESS QUIZ

- What makes your business (or you) different from your competition?

- What makes you better than your competition?

- What makes you and your organization unique?

- Brainstorm a high concept with your colleagues, then ask: "How does this differ from our competition? Are these the same things our customers would say?"

Four

THE POWER OF STORY

The old man turned to me and said, "Son, where do you suppose that I got the money to start my restaurant?"

I had never met the gentleman before, but I was familiar with him. I was only twenty-one years old and was trying to make intelligent conversation with him when he threw me a curve by asking the question. I respectfully replied, "Well, sir, I suppose you had some money saved up."

"Nope," he said, "not a dime."

"Okay," I tried again, "did you round up some friends to be investors?"

"I didn't have any money—and I didn't have any friends that had any money!"

"Did you take out a second mortgage on your house?"

He laughed. "Now, you're kidding me, aren't you?"

I laughed back. I didn't want him to know I hadn't been kidding.

"Give up?" he asked. I nodded. "My seed money to start my business was the entire sum of my first Social Security check. That's how it all got started." And Colonel Harlan Sanders continued to tell me the entire story behind the genesis of Kentucky Fried Chicken.

If I am in my car during the afternoon rush hour, one feature I like to catch on the radio is Paul Harvey's "The Rest of the Story." I love to hear the turns and surprises that the masterful broadcaster spins and weaves. The twist at the end is almost always startling. I can't wait to hear the next one.

People love to hear stories. That's what show business is about—and that's what *your* business should be about, too. Amazing power lies in the story of your organization . . . and you.

THE REST OF THE STORY

Tim has always had a gift. He's always been "the smart one"—the one who was more mature than others his age, the one to whom everyone else turned for advice and guidance. His father is a dentist with one of the most engaging personalities you could find. His mother gives him his determination and drive—and balance. His parents not only encouraged him to do important things; they expected it. Tim was destined for greatness.

While still in high school, Tim and a buddy decided their state school boards' laws should be changed. With the amount of taxpayer money needed to fund local schools in the state, Tim argued that only voters should be able to choose the boards determining how those funds would be spent. A local legislator agreed to help—but only if Tim and his friend would do the research and write the law.

Not only did they examine the statutes and author the legislation, they actively lobbied for its passage in both chambers of the state legislature. The bill became law, perhaps the only law in state history responsible for changing how the people are selected who impact over a billion dollars in state spending—and certainly the only one that was written by two high school seniors. When a reporter condescendingly asked Tim why he thought a bill written by a kid should even be considered, he answered, "It's the right thing to do. That shouldn't have an age limit."

After graduating second in his class at law school, Tim accepted a significant offer from a prestigious law firm and set about putting in the work necessary to become a partner. At a social function for the firm, Tim met the daughter of one of the most influential entrepreneurs and political figures in the state. The attraction was instant. He loved her magnetic personality; she loved his drive, determination, and potential. They married not long after they met, and a little after a year of marriage, the couple welcomed a new son to the family. Her father, impressed by his new son-in-law, encouraged Tim to give up his position at the law firm and come on board with the family business. Agreeing to the career change for many personal and professional reasons, Tim developed a plan to purchase a manufacturer of school buses. The company had fallen on hard times, but Tim's analysis concluded it could be turned around.

Tim then entered the most difficult time of his life. The school bus business is unlike most other companies for many reasons, not the least of which is that it is subject to the bidding process from local schools. In many cases, having a higher quality product doesn't matter; the only thing that wins you bids is if you can sell your product cheaper. Manufacturing, then, becomes governed in many cases by simple "economies of scale." The more you make, the cheaper you can sell them; the more you sell, the cheaper you can make them.

One of Tim's problems was that he was saddled with an unproductive manufacturing plant and challenges with the union. Even after he purchased a new plant and moved the company to another town—even buying out a competitor and merging operations—the difficulties continued to mount. However, the former CEO of the bus company Tim had purchased was a great new partner and friend. His expertise in manufacturing was second to none, and he helped Tim streamline the business.

Tim's company started receiving national attention for its progress. His creative marketing efforts and innovative work with the dealer network earned high marks from all concerned. Yet Tim knew some basic problems would probably never be solved because of the nature of the industry. The industry leader had such a significant advantage in the cost of production that Tim's company would never be able to build buses cheaper.

While he was running the business, he also wanted to do a good job for his father-in-law, whom he greatly admired. Given the amount of capital he had invested in the company, his father-in-law was a part of all of the major decisions Tim had to make. As a result, Tim's pressures were not only of a professional nature; they were intensely personal, as well. In addition, Tim's salary was less than it had been when he was working at the law firm several years earlier. He had been promised a significant share of the business he was running—but that business was in trouble.

Tim finally realized that the company was no longer economically viable without a greater infusion of capital than his father-in-law could commit. He went about the task of finding a buyer—and negotiated a sale that, given the circumstances, was highly favorable to his father-in-law. In the meantime, the stress and pressures of his job took a toll on his personal life.

The guy who was "destined for greatness" found himself with neither a job nor a wife. After spending a few nights in a friend's guest room, he moved from his huge, stately home into a one-bedroom apartment. While most people would have used the change in location as an excuse to surrender to life's circumstances, Tim, instead, vowed he would use his pain to mold himself into a lasting force in the business community. The apartment became his school. He read voraciously, studying how Warren Buffett had amassed his fortune and learning how mergers and acquisitions experts—like the firm KKR—had developed their strategies. He synthesized their wisdom and developed his own approach.

Tim decided he would buy companies, build their business, and then leverage that enhanced value to provide the capital to buy another, and another and another and another. Tim asked the people who still believed in him after his difficult experience with the school bus company to share in his new endeavor. And he rewarded them immediately with part ownership in the business.

Today, Tim looks out the window from a house he purchased on a beautiful lake and knows he would not be there if not for the challenges—and the solutions—found in a one-bedroom apartment. He says now that he would never buy a company that needs to be "turned around" for one simple reason: Most turnarounds don't happen. He has developed detailed strategies and mathematical models for which companies are financially attractive—and which aren't.

The lessons of the one-bedroom apartment are many; however, Tim would tell you four of the most important are:

1. Someone can take away your job and your company; *no one* can take away the power of your mind.

2. Mistakes are only profitable when you learn from them. Tim's highly successful philosophy of "Most turnarounds don't happen" is grounded in his experience.

3. Everybody needs a "one-bedroom apartment" where they learn, study, and refocus their lives.

4. To be truly successful, at some point you have to leave the apartment and *make* it happen.

You read earlier in this book a little bit about Tim Durham, my closest friend and CEO of Obsidian Enterprises. Now you know some of "the rest of *his* story." Please note that your *feelings* for the company are now richer, because you know that Obsidian isn't just based on good business practices. It's founded on experiences that are grounded in pain and tears.

I am still gratified that Tim asked me to be a co-owner, board member, and part of his company (and godfather to his son, Timothy Scott Durham). You'll read more later in this book about the Obsidian story. However, notice the power of this example: Tim Durham is now a successful businessman—and Obsidian has become a successful company—*because* of the trials and tribulations Tim has experienced.

Helen Keller once wrote, "The world is full of pain and suffering. It is also full of the *overcoming* of it."

STORYTELLING—YOUR MOST IMPORTANT SKILL

The Futurist is the leading publication for intellectuals who chiefly focus on future trends in the culture. In the August 1999 issue, one of the leading futurists of the world, Rolf Jensen, director of the Copenhagen Institute for Futures Studies, predicted what would be the most important skill a business could possess in the twenty-first century—the ability to create and relate stories. As Jensen puts it, "The challenge will be for all kinds of companies—whether producing consumables, necessities, luxuries, or services—to create the *story* behind their products."

We are overwhelmed with technology today. We need to find some method to take all the technical advances—and the products and services these advances have created—and make sense out of them. That is the fundamental role of the story in business. It creates the first method by which our audiences (customers, prospects, and

colleagues) understand and emotionally bond with us, organizationally and individually.

According to the magazine, "If Jensen is right, companies will
come to value storytellers not only in their creative advertising departments, but in executive positions, where refashioning a company's history and traditions into an appealing myth will be crucial for winning
the enthusiasm of employees, the affection of customers, and the
respect of the general public." Because of our entertainment culture,
stories are more powerful than ever. Our children learn many of the
basic things we take for granted, including values, arithmetic, and the
ABCs, from story skits on shows like *Sesame Street* and *Barney*.

The Coke legend, of course, is powerful and historic. The CEO is
entrusted with not only managing the business, but also with being
the shepherd of the story. The *Atlanta Journal* criticized the more
recent chairman Doug Daft with these words: "Daft seems not to
know the company's history." Even in today's high-tech, fast-paced
economy, it is not enough to be proficient at management. A true
leader paints vivid pictures of his or her organization's past—and
future—through stories that make emotional connections.

Even if you are running a little mom-and-pop store somewhere,
the power of emotion is in your story. If you stop reminding customers and prospective customers of your story, you give them one
more reason to go someplace else. Focus on your strengths—and
your uniqueness—and tell your story in a dramatic, visual manner.

Recently, Southwest Airlines, in conjunction with a milestone
anniversary, had several ads featuring its "mythology." According to
the story, cofounders Rollin King and Herb Kelleher got together and
decided to start a different kind of airline. Southwest said, "They
began with one simple notion: If you get your passengers to their destinations when they want to get there, on time, at the lowest possible
fares, and make darn sure they have a good time doing it, people will

fly your airline." Remember the high concept for Southwest Airlines we discussed in the last chapter? "Cheap. Safe. Fun." As the story is told by Southwest, King and Kelleher drew a triangle on a cocktail napkin. That shape represented the route map of the airline they had in mind, one that would begin by flying from Dallas to Houston to San Antonio. Southwest is an airline that started with only three destinations—and only three jets! In twenty-eight years, the company became the fifth largest major airline in America. It now flies more than 57 million passengers a year to 57 cities at 58 airports over 2,600 times a day

Companies will come to value storytellers not only in their creative advertising departments, but in executive positions, where refashioning a company's history and traditions into an appealing myth will be crucial for winning the enthusiasm of employees, the affection of customers, and the respect of the general public."

—*THE FUTURIST*

As you read this, many of you may be thinking, "Not *another* story about Southwest Airlines." I would gladly tell another carrier's story if one had circulated something as memorable as the story of how an airline started with just an idea and a drawing of a route map on a napkin. Having a "company story" is powerful and contributes to making an emotional connection with clients and colleagues.

Did you know, for example, that United Airlines traces its history back to a flight by pilot Leon Cuddeback on April 6, 1926, for Walter T. Varney, who initiated airmail service over an isolated stretch of land between Pasco, Washington, and Elko, Nevada? Didn't think so. I didn't either. But, it *would* make a great story—if only someone would tell it in a powerful, engaging manner.

Can you tell me the origins of US Airways? I can vaguely remember flying Allegheny Airlines when I was a kid. I recall Piedmont Airlines because they gave you the entire can of Coke. I know they formed elements of USAir—the company that became US Airways.

I know you won't have to guess which airline is more profitable. I am not saying it is the *only* reason by a long shot, but ask yourself, do you identify more with the airline started on a napkin or a conglomeration of carries you can't remember?

The best sales people are the ones who are passionate and excited about their product. They are the ones who are inspired and want to help you learn what they have discovered. The best sales people make an emotional connection through a story or a narrative.

Over the past few years, I have purchased three new cars from Carl Nielsen at Dreyer and Reinbold BMW in Indianapolis. The first time I was in the dealership, I, quite frankly, was not sold on BMWs. I was a Mercedes man and saw no reason to change. However, since the BMW dealership was on the way to the Mercedes dealership, my wife persuaded me to stop in. After seeing me drive up in my Mercedes, Carl immediately approached us. His appearance seemed more like that of a high-level corporate executive than the stereotypical automobile sales professional.

"Back when I was in high school," Carl began narrating, "I was one of those guys who loved working on anything mechanical. I loved to tear things apart—and put them back together—just for the fun of it. I loved the precision of something that was marvelously engineered."

At first, I honestly thought, *What does this have to do with a car?* Then, I noticed the passion and fervor with which he was telling me the story. His enthusiasm commanded my attention. He didn't tell a long, boring story—but what he told was powerful in its simplicity.

"I'll bet," he continued, "at one time or another I have had my head under the hood of just about every kind of car imaginable. I love the details." At that point I noticed some of the awards in his office; he had been recognized by BMW of America as one of the most technically knowledgeable sales professionals in the country.

"And," he continued, "I love cars. Do you like to drive?"

I told him *yes*. I spend way too much time on airplanes, and I really enjoy the chance to get behind the wheel of my car, turn the radio up loud, and just *go*.

"Get this," he exclaimed, "this past weekend, I got to drive one of our demo models three hundred miles to a BMW event!"

At this point, I was amazed. I mean, this guy spends all his working hours around these cars and he is still sincerely enthusiastic about spending a weekend behind the wheel of one.

He then told me, "Scott"—I noticed he remembered my name— "there are parts about your Mercedes that are better than the BMW. But I honestly believe there are aspects of the BMW that are so superior to what you are currently driving that if you will give me a chance, I can prove to you that you should be driving one of my cars."

As we went for the test drive, the story continued. He asked me if I had ever torn apart a brake assembly—which I haven't. We pulled

> # A story will stick in the listener's mind far longer than a list of facts or statistics.

over in a parking lot, and using his hands to represent brake drums, he explained how the brakes work and what they look like from the inside out. He explained the reasons he thought the BMW brakes were superior. Everything he said was connected back to the lessons he had learned tearing apart old cars in his yard as a high school kid. The mistakes he made on cars back then led to his current expertise.

Carl loves the technical aspect of the automobiles infinitely more than I ever will. But he was smart enough to make an emotional connection through the use of his story. The narrative was strong because it was personal, and convincing because he was knowledgeable about the subject. The connection allowed me to care about his mechanical knowledge to such a degree that it influenced my purchase decision. I have been hooked on BMWs for years now. But before I could get hooked on the car—*Carl Nielsen had to hook me with his story!*

Great stories create great mental images; they form mental pictures that emotionally bond us to events. You can *see* in your "mind's eye" Carl Nielsen working on a car and Tim Durham in his small apartment. Stories draw pictures for us that are infinitely more powerful than mere facts or abstract ideas. A story will stick in the listener's mind far longer than a list of facts or statistics. When people can "see" what we're saying, an emotional connection is made.

THE STORY AND HIGH CONCEPT

Notice in the Southwest example, the telling of the story was really an enhancement of the high concept discussed in the previous chapter. This follows the show business model:

- Develop a high concept
- Tell a Powerful Story
- Create the Ultimate Experience

You have already developed your high concept. Now it is time to create your story—the "screenplay," if you will—about what your organization, department, or you are all about. We love hearing corporate mythology—legends or traditions. We love hearing about how Hewlett-Packard started in a garage. Having a great story creates emotional bonding with customers and employees. Your customers and employees are starving for an emotional connection. You need to build on the high concept with a story that will engage them with you, allowing you to do much more than make sales. This story will help you build loyalty.

THE STORY AND IMAGE

When you convey your high concept through a compelling story, you are creating an image. People see you the way you present yourself, and the visual imagery created through a story creates a better impression than merely stating a fact. In other words, Hewlett-Packard could merely state that they are an inventive company, but it won't create the lasting impression that the story of an invention created by the entrepreneurs in a garage does.

Political figures who understand the power of the story do the same thing. According to public opinion polls, Ronald Reagan was one of the twentieth century's most popular presidents. His great success and popularity can be attributed, in large part, to his use of "show business" principles in the public sector. He told his story not just with words but through the image he presented to the camera. The members of the Reagan White House were masterful when it came to creating visual imagery for the evening news. A former White House staff member told me that the Reagan White House believed that every public appearance by the president gave them a chance to show and share Mr. Reagan's vision. Every Reagan public appearance was planned with the great care and meticulous nature of a movie set. The imagery made a much more powerful impression than the mere words Mr. Reagan used to communicate. People would remember what they saw on television more than they would remember the words that had been spoken, or the ideas that had been discussed. To truly be effective, the words—and the surroundings—both had to create powerful imagery.

Lenin said, "Capitalism thrives on the shrewd manipulation of imagery." Perhaps he realized that all business would become show business. Lenin obviously understood the power of stories and the importance that imagery plays in telling a story that emotionally connects with the intended audience.

ELEMENTS OF A GOOD STORY

Whether it is a movie, television program, or your corporate story, certain basic elements are found in all stories, even though there are many ways to express what is important. For example, in the book *How to Write and Sell Your Life Experiences,* Marjorie Holmes says the five fundamentals are: (1) a provocative idea; (2) appropriate style; (3) smooth, sound structure; (4) pertinent human anecdotes; and (5) a good clear summary or conclusion. In their work *Elements of the*

> # Your story must consist of these elements: (1) The hero, (2) A strong narrative tension, and (3) A memorable conclusion

Short Story, Kathleen Dinneen and Maryanne O'Connor of Yale-New Haven Teachers Institute conclude that good story writing should involve the elements of character, setting, plot, point of view, and theme. One of the most successful authors and lecturers on the subject is Bill Johnson; his book and seminar, *A Story Is a Promise*, suggest that a well-told story is both "a promise and a promise kept." Johnson's point is that you keep the promise through the interaction of the elements of stories—character, plot, theme, action, conflict, and resolution—to create the effect of dramatic fulfillment.

This is all well and good to keep in mind when you're writing your story, but don't get overwhelmed with all the elements. Since it's *your* story, it'll mostly fall into place: you're the hero and you know the trials and challenges you went through. Now, it is up to you to write about those challenges with a bold, descriptive tension that builds to a memorable finale to showcase your strengths. It'll boil down to a story that consists of these elements:

- A hero—your organization (or you) as described through the trials and challenges that have been overcome

- A strong narrative tension—something that will make your audience wonder what happens next

- A memorable conclusion—what your organization (or you) have learned from the trials and how that has made you stronger

Many times, individuals and organizations have difficulty creating compelling stories because they are unwilling to portray themselves as capable of mistakes, or as someone who was once on the "losing" side. Look back at the trials and challenges, the problems you faced that got you where you are today, and tell your story!

CRAFTING YOUR OWN STORY

If you don't take the initiative to tell your—or your organization's—story, someone else will. Your customers and colleagues really do want to know the story behind what you do. You don't want them to tell that story for you without your input. This is your chance to grab the world's attention and powerfully convey what makes you unique, with a story no one will ever forget.

Let's examine the elements that create a compelling business story.

THE HERO

No company has ever started because all the customers in a given industry were thrilled, prices were low, service was high, and all was peaches and cream. Businesses get started because of some kind of challenge, problem, or need. When a business solves the problem, they become the hero, and a story is born.

In 1996, Mark Begelman was a musician with a problem. A lead guitar player, Begelman felt that he—and musicians like him—were not being served well by local music stores. They didn't have the products he wanted at the time he wanted them. When they did have them, he was often told that in order to "try it, you have to buy it." Those stores that did allow him to play an instrument before purchase would always warn him to "keep it down." Imagine the challenges, problems, and frustrations musicians faced in 1996, encountering an industry with no national brand leader and 8,000 different dealers, all relying on an archaic method of distribution and fulfillment.

Begelman was not a corporate consultant or university professor looking at the situation from afar. He was just a guy—albeit a unique one—having a tough time finding guitar strings.

You have probably already guessed that this is the initial part of the corporate story of the MARS music store chain. Yes, Begelman is a musician; in fact, he is currently the lead guitar player in the company band Men from Mars. He also happens to be the chairman and CEO of the company that is doing well over $200 million in sales. Of course, Begelman had some business experience that the retail clerks who had snarled at him in the old music stores didn't appreciate. He was the president and chief operating officer of Office Depot. That fact only adds an extra dollop of interest to the story of his trials and challenges.

MARS music stores have solved a problem for many musicians and have, in a sense, become the hero of the story. The fact that Begelman, a fellow musician, faced a problem and, acting on his passion, overcame the problem says a lot. It tells a powerful story.

The most important writer on the power of stories is Joseph Campbell. He talks about the meaning and importance of myths—or legends—that are passed down from generation to generation. Through his early studies, Campbell discerned that there were similar elements in all myths. In his 1948 work, *The Hero with a Thousand Faces,* Campbell expounds on his concept of the "Hero's Journey"— a journey through rites of passage to final transfiguration.

One of Campbell's main points is that for the story to be compelling, the hero cannot begin the narrative as the winner. Only through trials and tribulations—being tested and defeated and then rising up to conquer—do we really have a hero. For instance, in Homer's *Odyssey*, Ulysses does not begin the book as a hero. It is through the experiences and difficulties he faces that he *becomes* one. The power of this story would be greatly diminished without the challenges Ulysses overcomes.

Let's think about a couple of the more recent "show business" examples we have previously explored. When Bruce Willis enters the skyscraper in *Die Hard*, he isn't a hero. He is when he leaves it, though, because of the power of the story. It's the same thing with Keanu Reeves in *Speed*.

As a culture, we are story junkies. We get hooked on good stories. Whether it's the fantasy of a soap opera, the reality-based *Survivor*, or the real-life business world, stories with heroes and villains intrigue us. Many professionals who wouldn't deign to follow a soap opera couldn't wait to turn on the television to follow the never-ending sagas of Microsoft and the Department of Justice, find out what was happening with Jack Welch and GE, or try to discover what Sumner Redstone would do next with Viacom.

Campbell's message rings true for those of us crafting a business story. Companies—and managers—who never admit mistakes, who never encounter tribulations, and who never seem to be anywhere but "on top" are boring and uninteresting. They do not compel us to give them our business in the first place, let alone become loyal customers.

THE STRONG NARRATIVE TENSION

What would have happened if early in the movie *Speed*, Keanu Reeves had said, "Hey, no problem. We should be able to get everybody off the bus in about ten minutes. There is absolutely nothing to worry about"?

Well, you and I both know that if he had said that, there would be no movie called *Speed*. Without the dramatic tension, we lose interest in the story.

We *want* to wonder what will happen next. We love to be thrilled by the hero's journey as he or she overcomes the odds. Notice in the story of Tim Durham, the tension grew when you saw him fail once; when he ended up without a job, divorced, and in a small apartment, you wondered what was going to happen to Tim. Many organizations do not pay enough attention to what happens in this part of the story. Remember Joseph Campbell's point: if there is no journey, there is no hero.

To build this kind of dramatic tension, most novels, plays, and movies are written in the "three-act" format. In a motion picture, you do not have an intermission between the acts, and the use of this format is seamless from the audience's perspective. In other words, the customers of the movie do not perceive the shift from one act to another, yet the film follows this format to build the audience's suspense.

ACT ONE

The first act is the "setup" or introduction. Here we are introduced to the characters with whom we will be spending the next couple of hours. We gain insight into what makes them tick. The first act is also where the fundamental conflict, question, or situation that must be resolved by the end of the movie is introduced. In the movie *Die Hard*, for example, this is where we meet Bruce Willis's character and the hostages are taken in the skyscraper. Through the first act, the conflict is set up (what will happen to the hostages), and we meet and begin to identify with the main characters. In the movie *Speed*, we meet the main characters, Keanu Reeves and Sandra Bullock, as well as the villain, Dennis Hopper, in the first act. The bomb is on the bus and the nightmare for the passengers begins.

ACT TWO

The second act of the movie is always the longest of the three acts. It deals with the effort to resolve the conflict established in act one through the actions of the characters with whom we've come to identify. In *Die Hard*, this is Bruce Willis's effort to rescue the hostages and the twists and turns that happen along the way. In *Speed* it is the effort to get the passengers off the bus, while making sure it doesn't go slower than fifty miles per hour.

In other words, act two is really the "story" part of the movie. It is the bridge from the introduction of the characters and the conflict to the characters resolving the conflict. It's where all the "good stuff" happens in the middle that makes you care about what happens in the end.

ACT THREE

Act three is the resolution of the conflict. It is Bruce Willis rescuing the hostages, killing the bad guy, and regaining the affection of his wife. In *Speed*, it is the fight on top of the subway train that wipes out the villain, and the rescue of Sandra Bullock. The same formula works for all kinds of movies. In *Saving Private Ryan*, for example, act three is not only where Tom Hanks's character loses his life, but where we also realize the old soldier at the beginning of the film is in fact Private Ryan.

For a romantic movie, the three-act concept works the same way. In another Tom Hanks film, *Sleepless in Seattle*, act one is where Hanks, a single father, ends up talking on a radio station because his young son makes the call. Meg Ryan hears him and has a strange connection with his voice and sincerity. (It introduces the characters and sets up the conflict: they have to get together.) Act two is all the things that happen to keep this couple—who should obviously be together—apart. (It is the effort by the characters to resolve the conflict.) Act three is the scene on the observation deck of the Empire State Building where our star-crossed lovers finally get it together, and they go on to "live happily ever after." (It is the heroic resolution—pass the Kleenex.)

Most companies have failed to see how this format creates a story that is more compelling and emotionally connecting. On the web site for MARS, act one—Mark Begelman's identification of the need in the music industry for the same type of retail merchandising he had pioneered in office supplies—sets up a great story. However, the rest of the story builds no dramatic tension. It is almost as if it ends by saying, "so then we got big and made money." You need to show through the power of your story *why* your business is more customer driven or would be a great place to work.

Given Mark Begelman's journey—one that will strike a chord (pardon the pun) of understanding in the heart of every musician—if prospective customers hear the story, they will assume MARS is a place where they can get their hands on all different types of instruments with knowledgeable, consistent help, and where they can get lessons at an affordable price. If MARS tells its high concept through its story, musicians will become interested in seeing what the stores are all about.

THE MEMORABLE CONCLUSION

In the movies (or TV or novels) there is almost always a well-defined, heroic resolution. The guy gets the girl; the warrior kills the evil force; the cowboy in the white hat wins the duel with the one in black. In real life, however, we seldom get to spike the ball after scoring the winning touchdown . . . or ride off gallantly into the sunset with the wind at our back.

> **We are often our own worst storytellers. We enjoy and repeat the myths of other corporations and professionals—and fail to see our own.**

Part of that is our fault. In this high-tech, high-stress time, we don't allow ourselves to revel in the achievements we have attained. We don't tell the story, even to ourselves. We simply hurry on to the next event, and we miss the satisfying ending that was waiting to be noticed. We fail to celebrate, and we also fail to communicate to the world the conclusion of our triumph.

We are often our own worst storytellers. By that, I mean that we will enjoy and repeat the myths of other corporations and professionals—and fail to see our own. Tim Durham has told me the legend of Warren Buffett more times than I can remember. Yet, during a recent conversation, he told me he could not believe an interesting story could be written about *him*.

As we try to understand our stories, part of our problem is that we hope the *final* chapter is not written for a long, long time. We don't want to think we've reached the end of the story. So, to create a compelling conclusion, try to think of it this way: *the end may be a beginning*.

The end of the MARS story is getting the business up and running across the nation so that MARS stores become great places to put your hands on instruments. We won't be interested in how many stores MARS opened this quarter if we don't get hooked by this part of the story. The end of the story I told about Tim Durham is really the beginning of Obsidian Enterprises. At that point, the hero of the story had completed the journey by marshalling his strengths in the time of his greatest adversity.

Notice in both examples, these companies grew from what they learned. We want to know that there is continued expansion and success. We will be interested in the number of stores or the amount of growth as a way to keep the storyline going—and to provide us with a sense that there may be a sequel (another great story) coming in the not-too-distant future.

LEARNING AND GROWTH

A part of the reason that Tim Durham's story is so satisfying is because you know he not only conquered his situation, he also learned from his experiences. As a kid I always heard the line that those who do not "learn from their mistakes are condemned to repeat them." The same is true in business—and when you try to tell your story, your problem becomes abundantly clear. If the hero is eternally trapped in his or her trials, eventually we lose interest. We want to see movement.

After reading Tim's story, we realize he has learned through his challenges:

- that most turnarounds don't happen

- that the power of mind and ideas transcend the current professional situation

- that everyone needs to make time to realign and refocus

- that one must first plan and then take action in order to see any results

Please note the story does two powerful things concurrently: first, it gives you a great lesson that you can apply to your benefit; and second, it connects you emotionally with Tim Durham and Obsidian Enterprises in a manner that will benefit both you and Obsidian. In other words, an emotionally satisfying ending doesn't only instruct . . . it *entertains*.

When Bruce Willis leaves the skyscraper at the end of *Die Hard*, we know he has learned from what he has endured. We also know (or assume) that because of his newfound knowledge, he will be a better husband and person—and therefore start living as heroically in the rest of the world as he did when he was inside the skyscraper. Why is a similar conclusion important for your business? Because without learning and growth, the Hero's Journey really isn't worth our trip.

VISIBLE STRENGTHS

If you follow the system outlined here, the ending will naturally focus on your current positive qualities. Carl Nielsen didn't tell about tearing apart cars in the yard and then become a tailor. He used his strengths to attain significant success in his chosen profession. You should play to your strengths as well. Even as your business changes and grows, don't lose your focus on what made you strong in the first place. Southwest Airlines is no longer running three planes to three cities—yet its story continues to drive home the point established by its high concept: Southwest Airlines is still "Cheap. Safe. Fun."

AN EMOTIONAL RESPONSE

Satisfying endings are emotional. We want to cheer as you spike the ball or ride into the sunset. It might not have felt that way when you did it in real life. Many times we're too busy taking care of what comes next to enjoy the success as much as we should. But despite how matter-of-fact *you* feel about your success, you need to tell your Hero's Journey so it has an emotional impact on your listener.

Perhaps you are writing a story about your organization that is ancient history in which you were not personally involved. If so, you need to make certain you use the techniques of the three-act format and the Hero's Journey to build to a memorable conclusion. We love to read stories that contain emotion—but when writing our own story we tend to neglect it. Don't settle for a dry recitation of facts. Find the drama—and the emotion—at the heart of your story.

If you build on your high concept to craft a powerful story, you can generate an emotional connection that will construct a bond between your prospective customer and the promise of your organization. That bond will not only win you customers . . . it will win you customers for life.

ALL BUSINESS IS SHOW BUSINESS QUIZ

- What is the "story" of your company, department, organization, and team?

- How about *your* personal and professional story?

- Are these stories congruent with your high concept?

- What is compelling about these stories for your audience?

- What was the situation that caused your company to be founded?

- What are the trials, challenges, and tribulations that your business (or founder—or you) have had to face and overcome?

- What about this story differentiates you from your competition?

~

FIVE

THE ULTIMATE CUSTOMER EXPERIENCE

Your high concept has been developed. Your story has been written and told. Now it is time to fulfill the commitment your organization has made through these statements. The next step is to shine the spotlight—*and sharpen the focus*—on the execution of your story so that you create experiences that will thrill and amaze your customers and employees. In other words, the high concept grabbed their attention; the story has emotionally connected them; now they want to see your play hit the stage—your movie light up the screen. It's time for you and your organization to deliver.

FINDING YOUR FOCUS

A few years ago, I had a presentation to give at an early morning meeting in Springfield, Illinois. Springfield is not a long drive from Indianapolis (where I lived at the time), and so I had dinner with my wife, packed one suit, one pair of shoes, one tie, and one shirt. I took off for Springfield and arrived at the hotel about 9:30 P.M. As I arrived in my room and began to unpack, a sudden thought hit me like a ton of bricks: I had brought the wrong shirt!

Unintentionally, I had packed a shirt with French cuffs—but I knew my cufflinks were still on my dresser back home in Indianapolis. Since I use a lot of gestures when I speak, not having cufflinks would be horrendous. I would make a broad, sweeping gesture, and my cuff would flap out. This would be *terrible!*

I had to find cufflinks. I ran down to the hotel gift shop, only to find it had already closed for the night. I dashed across the street to the Hilton to find their gift shop was closed as well. I raced back to my hotel and ran up to the bellman. "I have a terrible problem," I exclaimed. "I have *got* to find some cufflinks!"

"Are you kidding me? Where do you suppose you can get cufflinks in Springfield, Illinois, at 9:40 P.M. on a Tuesday night?"

"That's what I'm asking you!"

He thought for a moment. "The only places I can think of are Wal-Mart and Target department stores. They are both open until 10 p.m., but they're on the other end of town and it will take you twenty minutes to drive there. You might just make it."

I jumped in my car and raced over to Wal-Mart with five minutes to spare. Dashing into Wal-Mart, I asked the greeter at the front of the store, "Do you have cufflinks?"

"You might try over there in jewelry," he answered. When I darted up to the jewelry counter and made my request, the expression on the clerk's face told me everything I needed to know about their inventory. I dashed back to my car, jumped in, and made a beeline to Target. As I ran into the store, I heard the announcement that it was, "10 P.M. and customers must now bring their purchases to the front." I caught the eye of a sympathetic cashier and exclaimed, "Cufflinks!"

She pointed and shouted, "Men's Department!"

I sprinted back to the Men's Department and skidded up to the counter. Out of breath, adrenaline pumping, I practically screamed at the clerk, "Do you have *cufflinks?*"

"No."

Dejected, I turned away and said to myself, "Oh, no! What am I going to do?"

"Sir," the clerk called after me, "is it really important?"

I turned around and explained how I had driven over from Indianapolis, brought the wrong shirt, and was going to have to give my speech tomorrow without cufflinks.

She smiled and asked, "Well, why don't you just buy another shirt?"

Wow! It had never occurred to me to get another shirt!

There's the problem! The focus of many organizations is on the cufflinks instead of the shirt. On internal politics instead of incredible products. On information instead of innovation. On policies instead of people. Many organizations are so focused on the technical aspects of their product and the organizational politics within their business that the spotlight is directed internally rather than externally.

If you take your seat at your local movie theatre and watch as the film you have chosen appears on the screen—only to find that it is totally out of focus—what is your reaction? You immediately become a disgruntled customer. You don't care if the reason the film is out of focus is because the projectionist didn't thread it properly in the projector; or because the cameraman didn't film it correctly; or because there was a problem in the transfer process so the film was duplicated poorly. You only care about the result—the out-of-focus film, and you are infuriated!

Why is it so hard for many businesses to understand the need to focus on the way *their* customers look at them? If your focus isn't in the right place in your business, you will never be able to deliver on the promise of your high concept and story, no matter how brilliant they are. Take a look at the discrepancy in organizations between what they *say* the focus is—and what it *really* is. If you fail to sharpen your focus, you will most likely also fail to create amazing experiences your customers (and employees) will want to repeat. And you will not be competitive in the twenty-first century.

Paul Cole, global director of the customer relationship management team for Cap Gemini Ernst & Young, was quoted in the September 2001 issue of *Fast Company* magazine as saying that "Since the Industrial Age, we have been building a business model that was designed to help people create, produce, and deliver a *product* to the

The focus of many organizations is on the cufflinks instead of the shirt. On internal politics instead of incredible products. On information instead of innovation. On policies instead of people. Many organizations are so focused on the technical aspects of their product and the organizational politics within their business that the spotlight is directed internally rather than externally.

market. But that business model wasn't designed to deliver an enhanced customer *experience*. Until we get marketing, sales, and customer service converging in a way that adds value, we're going to keep disappointing the ultimate customer."

The show business model keeps us from continuing to disappoint our customers and employees because it is designed to focus on the delivery of the experience. Let me give you an example from the experience of Pyramid Coach, one of the companies owned by Obsidian Enterprises.

Pyramid Coach is a company that leases many of the buses on which celebrities and bands travel to perform at concerts. When we bought the company, we decided we needed to totally revamp the interiors of all our coaches so they would be more dazzling to our celebrity clientele (as only made sense from an "ALL Business Is Show Business" perspective). That move seemed obvious to us. If you are a big-time country music star—as many of our clients were—we assumed you would want the most amazing accoutrements possible.

Fortunately, though, before we took any action, we talked to country music stars . . . and, even more important, we *listened* to them as well. What we discovered surprised us. Sure, they all wanted a nice bus in which to ride from show to show, a bus that had the feeling of home so they could relax during their hectic travel schedules. However, what they wanted more than anything else was a friendly, upbeat, reliable bus *driver*. They wanted someone behind the wheel who could be a part of their team—almost a member of the family.

We still decided to spend money creating innovative and remarkable interiors for our buses; after all, in many cases customers do judge quality by appearance. However, our investment in the interiors was much smaller than we had originally planned. We decided instead to make a larger investment in hiring, training, and providing incentives for drivers so we would have the best in the industry. (And I think we do!)

When you are in the bus business you might easily assume the buses matter most. When you are in show business, however, you understand that the delivery of the experience is firmly rooted in focusing on emotional connections—and what we found out was that the bus driver is far more essential to those connections than the fancy interiors.

In business, we tend to fixate on the technical aspects of the product we have created. This is only natural; we have been trained for years to focus primarily on how our goods and services are engineered, manufactured, and distributed. And when we study organizational behavior, we find we have also become highly "system oriented." Managers are trained to develop and administer systems that enhance the efficiency of their organization.

Unfortunately, this orientation does not mirror what has been happening in society as a whole. As we have already discovered, as a culture we have become much more "emotionally oriented." One of the challenges we face as we try to enhance our customers' experiences is that most of us are coming from a systems perspective, while the customer is coming from an emotional one. If you want to revise your business orientation—and sharpen your focus—you need to build the Ultimate Customer Experience (UCE).

DEFINING *ULTIMATE*

When you think of the word *ultimate* you usually think of the best or most extreme. "It was the ultimate flying machine" or "It was the ultimate weekend getaway." The word *ultimate* can also mean the fundamentals or the basics, as in, "It is the ultimate purpose of our business." When I say that you should create an *Ultimate* Customer

Experience, I'm saying that it should be a fundamental to your company, but it should also be the best and most extreme experience you can give your customer.

Let's begin to think about the ultimate experience a customer could enjoy with regard to your product or service. What would move the experience beyond mere ordinary . . . to extraordinary . . . to ultimate? When customers have an experience that is flat-out amazing, they experience the emotional connection needed to build loyal customers.

For years I have been telling people about the great service I have received from Nordstrom in Indianapolis. Nordstrom's is often cited in "customer service" books as being a leader in the field. They do an incredible job. For the longest time I wouldn't even consider buying a suit anywhere else. And then I met Steven King.

When first introduced to Steven King, I said to him, "You don't look like Steven King." He replied—as I am certain he has a million times—"I'm the tailor, not the writer. He has more money . . . I have better suits." He went on to tell me that he had been hearing from his customers about how much I loved Nordstrom—and he wanted to make me a little wager. "I'll bet you I can get you a better suit for the same price and provide even better service than you are getting from Nordstrom." I almost didn't take the bet, because I did not want to take money from such a poor, misguided soul. He obviously did not know how satisfied I was by my Nordstrom experience.

Well, I was the one who was wrong, and Steven has now made several phenomenal suits for me. But the important part of this story resides in the details. When I arrived at Steven's store—I went to visit him even though he offered to come to my house with a tape measure and fabric—I was amazed at the variety and the look of the suits. His racks offered anything from highly contemporary to very businesslike—ties, casual shirts, shoes, and everything else the well-dressed gentleman would want. As I looked around the store, I was amazed to see as many suits on display as you would find in a large department store—and an almost infinite number of fabrics from which to choose. Then Steven came out and asked me a question I'd never before been asked in a men's clothing store: "Hey, want some coffee?" In the relaxed atmosphere his offer had created, Steven next asked me about my speeches, how I packed for travel, and if my occupation required any special considerations.

"Well," I told him, "there is one thing that may sound kind of strange. Because I use gestures so much as a part of my speaking style, my sleeves always seem too short."

Steven smiled. "We can fix that. Stand up and let's measure you."

We were well on our way to one of those flat-out amazing, ultimate customer experiences. Unlike buying a suit off the rack, where sizes can vary slightly between manufacturers, Steven's shop, The King's Image, now has my measurements stored in its computer; that means they can recreate the fit exactly every time. They'll bring swatches of fabric for me to view, so all I need to do is pick the color and feel I want. Then they will have a perfectly tailored, custom-made suit delivered to me relatively quickly and all at the same price I was paying at Nordstrom. While the giant retailer operates in a beautiful downtown mall, The King's Image is more modest. You do not have to be a huge business to apply the "ALL Business Is Show Business" principle.

Tour de France winner Lance Armstrong's recent book is titled *It's Not About the Bike*. That's a message Steven King understands. He knows his business is not just about the suit. Sure the fit, the feel, and the fabric are important, but the finesse and friendship really make the Ultimate Customer Experience. Remember this principle: Friends don't want to fire friends. When you receive an Ultimate Customer Experience and are emotionally connected, loyalty becomes a part of the package.

RAISING THE STANDARD

The first time we receive an "ultimate" experience we are excited. The next time we experience the "ultimate" we are happy. Eventually, we become content and expect such an experience to the point where it becomes mundane. Then we want to be wowed all over again, taking our expectations to a new level. Customer expectations are always changing and are today at an all-time high . . . and rising! As times change, people change. The "ultimate" of a few years ago won't cut it in today's marketplace.

One of the problems fast food businesses like McDonald's and Burger King encounter is that their success has "spoiled" their customers. By consistently providing fast food, what was remarkable just a few years ago now seems to be pretty ordinary; no one is impressed anymore.

Utility companies face a similar problem. When was the last time you were impressed that your phone was working? The telephone service that was considered simply amazing earlier in this century is now taken for granted. The only time you notice the phone is when it does *not* work. How does a business facing those kinds of customer experiences move into the realm of a UCE?

Of course, if you're the phone company or a fast food chain—or any of the other number of businesses who find themselves in a similar predicament—this doesn't seem fair. You know how hard you and your colleagues work to create a product and service that is reliable and dependable with great value for your customers. But despite all your efforts, you are rewarded with customers who are bored. The problem is, business—like life—simply isn't fair.

It would be wonderful if customers recognized your efforts on their behalf. Customers, though, are generally blind to any perspective but their own. When you are a customer, are *you* any different? If you drive through McDonald's, for instance, and they tell you to pull over and wait for your order, do you say, "No problem. In my business, I understand how unrealistic customer expectations can be and I'm perfectly willing to wait"? No! You rev your motor so they'll recognize your impatience and bring the Big Mac a little quicker.

In his recent book *Real Time*, Regis McKenna states that we must prepare for "the age of the never satisfied customer." While I certainly agree with the premise that customers are getting harder to please, I would take a different approach and suggest that customers should not be merely satisfied—they should be amazed, astounded, and thrilled. If they don't experience something at least close to a UCE, we will lose their business. If our customers are "never satisfied," it is *our* fault!

But the challenge we face is not an impossible one. If companies like Nordstrom, Nike, Starbucks, Disney, FedEx, and others can create UCEs on an international level, while lesser-known companies like the King's Image do it locally, then clearly customers *can* be satisfied. If the bar keeps rising, then we simply need to jump higher.

ELEMENTS OF A UCE

The Ultimate Customer Experience will obviously vary from industry to industry, even from company to company. The UCE for the purchase of a car, for example, will have elements that differ from those of a fast food restaurant. Despite these differences, however, five common elements are the same no matter what your product or service. Using these elements, you will be able to see how you can begin to shape the specific experience your customers want. An Ultimate Customer Experience must:

• Deliver on the promise made by your story.

- Create emotional bonds between the organization and the customer.

- Be based on the customer's point of view.

- Be repeatable and measurable.

DELIVERING YOUR STORY'S PROMISE

How would you feel if you booked a flight on Southwest Airlines and found the ticket was more expensive than other airlines? Or if your FedEx package shows up three days late? Or if the Domino's pizza you ordered last night arrives in time for breakfast? Or if you rent the movie about a "bomb on a bus" only to find that this version of *Speed* is about a middle school track team?

Are these scenarios silly? Perhaps. But these events would be no less discouraging than waiting in line at a fast food restaurant that had unhelpful employees and messy tables all the while proclaiming that "The Customer is Number One!"

If your high concept says the package is going to get there overnight, it had better do so. If your high concept says you will "fly people through financial turbulence," then you had better be on the phone with them when the market dips. The high concept is there not only to grab attention but also to make a distinction between your organization and its competitors. If the customer experience doesn't substantiate the differentiation, then you certainly can't say it was ultimate.

Late one night as I checked into a hotel, I noticed a sign at the front desk that stated, "Your Total Satisfaction or Your Room Is Free." I remarked to the desk clerk that the guarantee seemed to be pretty impressive. His response was to shrug his shoulders and mumble, "Yeah."

When I got to *my* room, I inserted the plastic key card into the slot on the door, only to hear someone inside the room shout, "Who is it?" I stammered, "Sorry! They must have given me the wrong key at the front desk." Dragging my bone-tired body back down the elevator and back to the desk, I waited while the clerk finished up a personal call; then I coldly told him he had assigned me a room that was already occupied.

"Sorry, dude."

Now I had a new room assignment. So back up the elevator I went, to another room. This time the key worked perfectly—but when the door swung open, I saw an unmade bed, dirty towels strewn everywhere, and two ashtrays filled with cigarette butts (even though it was listed as a nonsmoking room). Back down to the front desk, back to the desk clerk, who by this time was dozing off in his chair. "Excuse me," I said through clenched teeth, "*this* room hasn't been cleaned."

An Ultimate Customer Experience must: Deliver on the promise made by your story; Create emotional bonds between the organization and the customer; Be based on the customer's point of view; Be repeatable and measurable.

"Oh, man," he replied, "is our computer screwed or what?" In icy silence I watched as he got another room for me. Handing me the key, he made an attempt at humor. "Third time's the charm, right, dude?"

"It had better be—dude," was my steely response. As I entered the room, there, on top of the television, was a laminated sign that said, "Your Total Satisfaction or Your Room Is Free."

The next morning, I asked to see the manager. I described my problem, clearly explained my dissatisfaction, and then pointed to his high concept sign. "I am assuming you will make this right?"

His response—which stunned me—was, "Well, after you got to the clean room, was it satisfactory?"

"That's not the point," I replied.

"Yes, it is. You were satisfied with the room you ended up with. It's not right if you don't pay us for it." Needless to say, I was now an irate customer. The fast-thinking manager proposed a solution. "Hey, what if I give you a room free the next time you stay with us?" There was not a "next time," of course.

Don't promise, "Your Total Satisfaction or Your Room Is Free" if you aren't going to give me the room free when I'm not satisfied. Make your high concept, instead "A One Out of Three Chance You'll Get the Right Room." But if you say it—do it. Carry out your high concept to build your UCE. Period. If you don't you'll only be shooting yourself in the foot. With your eyes on the quick buck, you'll lose the chance to do business in the future.

Your story—which is told by you, your organization, your employees, and your advertising—is a *promise* you are making to your customers. You must "keep the faith" and deliver on your commitment. Unfortunately, many companies have moved away from their stories. When a company starts in a garage and builds its corporate myth on the image of independent innovation—yet becomes an organization that is stale and bound in bureaucracy—it has failed both its customers and its employees.

Think of companies that deliver on their promise every single day. One that occurs to me immediately is McDonald's. You might phrase the McDonald's high concept as "make every customer in every restaurant smile." With a high concept like that, is it any wonder that McDonald's has created a clown to be its spokesperson?

As it has built its story over the years, we as customers understand the promise McDonald's makes to us is that it will make us smile—by providing service, quality, cleanliness, and value in a timely manner. The more we know about the McDonald's story, the more we realize that all its efforts are centered around making the story come true for millions of customers on a daily basis. Does McDonald's always provide a UCE for their customers? Of course not. However, it *is* working on it.

Driving from Los Angeles to Fresno for a speech, I was struck by a "Big Mac Attack." Noting the famous golden arches not far in the distance, I pulled into the familiar fast food restaurant. I walked inside and ordered my Big Mac. And then I said, "Oh no!"

The friendly clerk asked, "What's the matter?"

"Oh," I replied, "I'm going to have to change my order. I can't have that Big Mac I've been wanting."

"Now, why in the world can't you get that Big Mac you're craving?" she asked.

"My doctor has me on a new diet," I answered. "I can't eat sesame seeds."

"Wait right there," she commanded. She practically jogged back to where the sandwiches were prepared, whispered something in the ear of her colleague making the Big Macs, smiled, waited for a second, then came back to me with a sandwich wrapped and ready.

"Here you go!" she exclaimed.

"But I shouldn't—" I started to object.

She smiled. "Just take a look at it."

I opened the wrapper to find two all-beef patties, special sauce, lettuce, cheese, pickles, and onions—on a bun that was really two bottoms with *no* sesame seed top. With a look as solemn as a president speaking to Congress, she said, "No one should ignore a craving for a Big Mac."

You can bet McDonald's made me smile that day. And the promise of the story—built on the high concept—was fulfilled. I received a UCE.

CREATING EMOTIONAL BONDS

We've already talked a great deal about the importance of creating an emotional connection between the customer and your organization. No UCE will work without that emotional element. There are many ways to create an emotional bond—and the determining factors are as varied as your customer base. Some of them include:

- The quality of your product or service
- The price of your product
- The lifespan of your product
- How your product or service is marketed and distributed
- How your product or service is delivered
- The experience and training level of your employees
- The uniqueness of your competitors

No matter what your product or service is, there *is* an appropriate emotional response. For example, what is the appropriate emotional response at McDonald's? Based on our earlier understanding of McDonald's high concept and story, the emotional response should be smiling and joy. To create the UCE, this product should be delivered with speed of service and at a reasonable price. Meanwhile, the appropriate emotional response at Benihana's Japanese steak house will be quite different. Certainly, joyful smiles are a part of the experience this establishment wants to create as well. But as customers, we'd be pretty disappointed if all we got was a hamburger and a paper packet of French fries; the emotional connection at Benihana's is a great show that includes the meal. By the same token, we don't want the speedy service we demand of McDonald's for a UCE at Benihana's; we want to savor not only the food but also the total dining experience. We want the artistry of the chef as he cooks the meal, the costumes of all of the wait staff, the fun that is involved with eating a dinner there.

Don't overlook the little things. Knowing the customer's name, knowing what they like and what they want, knowing how many kids they have and their ages—all of these seemingly "little" things mean big emotional connections.

When I speak on behalf of Conseco Fund Group to their clients all over the country, I always tell financial advisors to remember one very important detail: To build a relationship, your clients must know you care more about them than their money. Take the same principle and apply it to your own situation: to make an emotional connection, *your* clients must know you care more about them than their business.

Driving from a speech in New Jersey to make a flight at LaGuardia Airport in New York City, I was admiring the sights of the city as I drove across the George Washington Bridge for the first time in my life. Suddenly, the truck in front of me slammed on his brakes and came to a screeching halt, while the surrounding traffic continued to move normally. Standing on my brakes, I realized I was not going to stop in time. I braced for the collision . . . the air bag exploded in my face . . . and the car came to a shuddering halt. My Hertz rental car was practically totaled.

After a moment of stunned stillness, I realized I was physically fine. I pried open my door and ran to the truck I had hit; I was relieved to see the driver was not hurt. Returning to my wrecked car, I called 911 to report the accident. Then I called the emergency number at Hertz to let them know what had happened.

The operator immediately asked, "Mr. McKain, are you okay?"

"Yes," I said, "I'm fine."

"Sir," she replied, "to be honest—you don't sound fine. Are you certain you are all right?"

I took a deep breath and responded, "I am a little shaky. But physically I am not injured at all."

I heard her exhale over the phone. "That's great," she said softly. "You know, we can always get another car. We can't get another Mr. McKain."

At that moment, an emotional connection was established for life between Hertz and me. She showed that Hertz—at that moment in my life, she *was* Hertz—cared more about my health than their car.

Author and professional speaker Jim Rohn once said, "That which is easy to do is also easy not to do. That's why most people don't do it." It should be easy to understand that we have to do the little things—asking our customers if they are okay before worrying about the automobile, for example—to make the big things work. Yet these little things seem so easy, most organizations neglect to do them; they assume that easy means unimportant.

An Ultimate Customer Experience *must* build emotional bonds.

THE CUSTOMER'S POINT OF VIEW

When do people begin their experience with your organization? It's not just when they are in front of you, but when they first come into contact with your organization. That may mean when they first call for directions, when they first pull into the parking lot, or when they are greeted by the doorman or receptionist. Their experience begins when *they* say it does.

Recently, I gave a presentation to a financial service group. At the meeting, we discussed the importance of the UCE—and the fact that the experience starts when the customer's contact with your organization begins, *not* necessarily when they are physically in front of you. I asked the group to think of a trip to an exquisite restaurant: if the valet parking attendant scratches your car, the hostess is surly, you are seated at a rotten table, and the restrooms are dirty—but the food is amazing and your waiter's service is outstanding—have you had an ultimate customer experience? Of course not. The problem, I told them, is that the waiter probably thinks you *did*! Why? Because from his perspective everything was executed to perfection. Unable to see the rest of your experience, he only sees what is in front of him, while *you* (the customer) have a different perspective.

Not long after that presentation, I received a call from one of the stockbrokers in attendance. He said he had been thinking of what I said while he analyzed the portfolio of a client, a widow who is over seventy years old and who doesn't come into the city very often. After thinking about developing a UCE for this client, the stockbroker realized that *his* experience began when she was in his office discussing her financial matters while *her* experience began when she pulled her car into the parking garage and started her trek to his office. First, she had to park in the garage in the skyscraper that housed the financial institution's offices. Then, she had to walk alone through the garage to the elevator to the building's lobby. From there, she had to walk through the lobby to the elevators that carried her to the office of her stockbroker.

When she stopped by his office the next day, he decided to begin to create a UCE for her. This time instead of walking her to the office lobby, or even to the building elevator, he took the experience to the ultimate level. He rode the elevator down to the building lobby, then walked her through the lobby to the parking garage elevator, rode that elevator with her down to her floor, walked her to her car, took her keys and opened the door, and assisted her into the car. He created the ultimate experience for her—from *her* perspective.

Before she backed out of her parking space, she lowered her car window and told the stockbroker she would be moving over to him $300,000 she had invested at another brokerage.

"You know," he told me, "I have studied finance and investing. Yet the UCE is one of the most powerful tools I have encountered in my profession. The only thing that bothers me is that I haven't been using it all along."

If you are going to create a UCE from your customers' perspective, then you need to understand what is important to your customers. But don't be too quick to think you know what that is. (We'll discuss this more in chapter six.)

Every time I speak to stockbrokers, someone in the audience will always say, "Wait. What my clients really want is performance." Well, no kidding! What client in his right mind is going to tell his broker otherwise? No client is going to say, "Hey, don't worry about making me any money. Just walk me through the lobby and open my car door." *All* clients and customers want you and your products and services to perform. A lot of businesses and organizations provide products and services that can perform to reasonably acceptable standards. It is what you do *beyond* that point that is a differentiating factor. And that is where you will forge emotional connections as well. So if you're not sure what your customers want, try this simple technique: *ask them!*

REPEATABLE AND MEASURABLE

Every organization should strive to create a UCE for all customers, every time they are in contact with the organization. The only way in which that can be accomplished is to structure the UCE so it is easily repeatable. You don't want your UCEs to be serendipitous flukes. The only way you can insure your UCEs will be repeated is to measure them.

For example, when the kind woman at Hertz told me she cared about me more than the car, that comment created a UCE for me. Great for Hertz—for that one instance. If you're Hertz, the challenge then is how to create those same emotionally bonding moments for every customer, every time by educating all their employees working the "Accident Desk" to respond in a similar manner. Let's say Hertz has developed a repeatable structure for their UCE. The next step is to make sure it is actually performed whenever staff members are dealing with real customers in real situations. The only way to make certain the structure is repeated is to measure it.

Once you are measuring your UCE, a way to make certain the experience is repeated is to reward your employees for doing so. Sounds simple, I know, but this is another point that is often overlooked or underestimated.

One of my all-time favorite business books is titled simply *GMP*. These initials stand for "Greatest Management Principle." The book was later released in paperback under the title *Getting Results*, and the author is noted business writer Dr. Michael LeBoeuf. Michael is one of our most insightful business scholars, and, I am proud to say, a close friend. His "Greatest Management Principle" is so simple and powerful yet often neglected: *Behavior that is rewarded will be repeated.*

Bounce that sentence around in your mind a few times. It sounds easy, doesn't it? But ask yourself—how many times do we instead reward behavior we do *not* want to see repeated? Auto manufacturers, for example, offer rewards called "rebates" to such an extent that they have "trained" their customers to wait and not buy a car unless deep discounts are being offered. What began as a way to stimulate sales has become a way to create price buyers. The behavior rewarded (get the rebate if you buy the car) becomes behavior repeated (wait until the next rebate to buy a car). Sometimes the behavior you reward is not the behavior you want.

Many managers tell employees that their bonuses will be based solely on goals tied to targets on stock price and profits. So the employees pay attention to the daily share price and margins—and forget about emotional connections with customers. Behavior rewarded is behavior repeated. Then the customers go away because they feel ignored—and everyone at the company blames the economy.

You cannot provide your customers with a UCE if you aren't rewarding employees for doing so. GMP works for customers as well as employees. Rewarded customers repeat their business when they receive a UCE. As you develop your Ultimate Customer Experience, you should also put a system into place to reward those who refer you and your organization. To make the reward significant, make it important enough to be desired.

Several of the old-time professional speakers—those who were on the "circuit" back in the 1950s—tell the story of one company that had a special reward for their best customers. All the top customers were invited to come to a lavish dinner—and bring their wives. (This was back when all the customers of this particular company were businesses owned by males.) After the couples were wined and dined, a professional speaker would come on stage to motivate, congratulate, and entertain.

Then something amazing would happen. The owner of the company sponsoring the dinner would get up and give a little speech directed at the customers. "Gentlemen," he would begin, "all of you have been wonderful customers. That's why you are here. We are grateful and we want to continue to grow together. However, one customer has done more business than the others—only, by the way, by a small margin—but we want to recognize our very best customer with a special prize."

The best customer—picture a guy in a suit with a skinny tie and black horn-rimmed glasses—is called up on the stage and given his reward: a lady's full-length mink coat!

The first time I heard this story, I have to admit I didn't quite get it. Then speaker Charles Willey—now in his eighties—explained, "Think about it. This guy waves for his wife to run up on the stage where he puts this mink coat around her and spins her to the crowd. Every wife in the audience is clapping but at the same time elbowing her husband and whispering through clenched teeth, 'That had better be *me* up there next year, Buster!'" How many orders do you suppose were placed the next day?

That's a creative reward!

When I was a little boy in Crothersville, Indiana, I would get my hair cut at the one and only barbershop in town. After every haircut, Dwight Sweazy, the barber, would pull out a big box of Tootsie Roll Pop suckers and offer me my choice of flavors. As a kid in that barber's chair I learned something that is very easy to forget in today's fast-paced business world: No transaction between a business and a customer is truly "ultimate" unless the customer receives some kind of reward for his or her patronage. Behavior rewarded *is* behavior repeated, so rewarded customers create *additional* sales *and* referrals—and more customers who can enjoy the ultimate experience you create for them.

DEVELOPING YOUR OWN UCE

Now that you know what all UCEs must contain, it is time to get started developing your own UCE system. All Ultimate Customer Experiences must be unique and tightly focused to the specific needs of your customers and the specific assets of your organization.

Sometimes organizations seek outside consulting for fresh eyes, ears, and minds as a part of this process. One of my companies, Experience Consulting Group (www.experienceconsultinggroup.com), helps organizations through the three-step process of high concept, story, and UCE. Other industry-specific consulting firms, PR firms, advertising agencies, and sales training groups can also be valuable resources.

However, whether you use outside experts or not, I cannot overemphasize the importance that you *do it*—create a UCE! A high concept and story that is never produced into a UCE for customers is exactly like a high concept and screenplay that sits on a shelf and never is produced into a movie—or the book that was written and never published.

Here are three steps you can take to develop your organization's UCE:

- Experience feedback

- Experience audit

- Experience brainstorming

EXPERIENCE FEEDBACK

As you formulate your UCE, customers must be involved. Find ways to ask your customers to give you the feedback you need to create the experience they want.

In show business, feedback comes from critics, audiences at plays, ratings on television, and ticket sales, while in publishing, book reviews plus the sales of any particular book provide feedback. Moviegoers often choose which feature they will see on any given weekend based on word of mouth, noticing lines at theaters, and watching facial expressions and body language as people walk out of the film. These forms of feedback are vitally important to any film's success. That is why movies often have "sneak previews." The studios will try to generate as much feedback as possible to ascertain what changes they need to make in a product before it is released to the general public; they also hope to build positive "word of mouth."

Obtaining customer feedback is probably tougher for your business. However, while it may be more difficult, it is every bit as important. To create the UCE you desire, product and service development must be ongoing. Learning what your customers think *and* *feel* about your product or service is vitally important in this show-business culture.

Many times in seminars and consulting assignments, I will ask if an organization is receiving quality customer feedback. As you might imagine, the answer is usually one hundred percent "yes." Then I ask—"So when was the last time you personally asked customers how you could provide them with the ultimate experience any customer could receive in your industry?"

The affirmative answer then drops by a significant percentage.

My friend George Walther, in his book *Upside Down Marketing*, tells the story of the time that he and I, as well as several other professional speakers, were on a cruise. As we were nearing our final port, the staff of Carnival Cruises gave us evaluation forms and told us that they should all be filled out with "excellent" as the score. "If you don't feel that a particular area has been up to par," they explained, "go ahead and mark it 'excellent' and then tell us personally what went wrong and we'll make it up to you."

Do you think Carnival believes they are getting good customer feedback? Yes, they probably believe it. My experience, however, tells me that they aren't.

The way you generate feedback will vary depending on your product or service. The important thing is to get feedback—and then don't be defensive; be willing to learn! Most customers don't want a hassle. But if customers know we truly want their input, they want to help us help them. What customer doesn't want a UCE? A friend of mine told me that after speaking with one of his customers about this not long ago, the client told him she appreciated his asking for her feedback. She smiled and told him, "You've got more of my business—because you've asked my opinion."

EXPERIENCE AUDIT

At movie sneak previews, the director and producers of the film will often attend the screenings (sometimes even in disguise) and sit with the audience to see how the production works in front of their customers.

When was the last time you went to Wal-Mart and watched customers look at your product? When was the last time you were a mystery shopper for your own products or services? If managers would call their own customer services lines and have to wait forever, trapped in "voice mail jail," those truly committed to UCE would make changes.

Not long after Tim Durham became CEO of a major school bus manufacturer, he asked many of their customers what they should improve about the school buses that they constructed. Some school bus drivers from rural areas told him they didn't like their buses because they had a dust problem. When Tim asked what that meant, they described how, on unpaved roads, a great deal of dust would enter the interior.

Tim returned to his office and called in his engineers. They responded, "No way. We build them to specifications that wouldn't allow that."

Rather than argue, Tim took a couple of the engineers, traveled to a small town in Indiana, got on a bus, and rode an after-school route. On a hot day with kids packed in the bus, the vehicle started to fill with dust. The engineers—used to their air-conditioned offices where they only saw the buses on the asphalt pavement of the plant—now had to endure the customers' experience.

"Guys," Tim asked them as they bounced along the unpaved road, "would you put up with this every day?" They looked down and shook their heads. "Then our customers shouldn't have to either." The engineers went to work to solve the problem.

After a conference for chiropractors, I received an e-mail from one who said he had noticed weeds were growing around the steps to his office. Hurrying in every morning with his mind on work, he had honestly never noticed them before. He realized his patients couldn't be having a UCE if they had to step over weeds to get to him. When he had the weeds pulled and the area landscaped, every patient mentioned it to him. Unfortunately, some even said, "I wondered how good a doctor you could be when you couldn't take care of your front steps."

In my early career in sales, I would go to drive-thrus and eat in the car as I hurried from one appointment to another. Throwing the bags in the back seat, I would rush to talk to another client or prospect. One time, a customer, who was signing an order standing by my car, looked in the back seat and asked me, "Are you going to take better care of my order than your car?"

Customers notice everything! We may want them to notice only products or services—instead they notice weeds and Burger King bags. Audit the experience your customers are receiving so you can build a UCE.

EXPERIENCE BRAINSTORMING

As you brainstorm, keep asking everyone this question: "And beyond that?" To get to the *ultimate* experience, you have to be willing to go beyond how most people and most organizations think. When someone proposes an idea during this brainstorming exercise, we want him or her to also go at least one step further. When you come up with an acceptable way to treat customers and show them that you value them, then you must ask yourself what you should do beyond that. And beyond that. And beyond that. Keep your customer in mind—what they need—when deciding what to do "beyond that." It takes going above and beyond the call of duty to create the Ultimate Customer Experience.

To use the earlier example of my accident, let's say that Hertz wants to make a similar emotional connection in all accident situations. They train their accident people to first ask about the welfare of the customer, but they don't stop there. Then, they should ask themselves what they should do "beyond that."

If the renter is not okay, of course we would get them the emergency assistance they need. But, if they are okay, but the vehicle is not, they're going to need another rental car or a ride somewhere.

"And beyond that?"

Find out where they are and provide transportation away from the scene of the accident.

"And beyond that?"

Help in filling out accident report forms.

"And beyond that?"

Some may be a little sheepish about renting again from us since they damaged a car. We want to keep their business, so we have to find a way to let them know they are valued Hertz customers.

Notice how all these steps build to create an Ultimate Customer

Experience—something that differentiates your organization and connects emotionally with the customer to build lifetime loyalty.

BE WILLING TO CHANGE!

If you aren't providing UCEs to your customers, you do not need to start working harder on the old plan. You need to shake things up!

As elementary as this sounds, you'd be surprised how many organizations do not "get it." If your customers aren't receiving a UCE—and you have become committed to providing one—then you are going to have to change something to make it happen.

Dole, for instance, is in a very traditional business based on fruits and vegetables. How many ways are there to market lettuce? Let's face it; changing the distribution channel is not a highly viable alternative. Most people are going to buy their lettuce at the supermarket. Dole, however, brainstormed to find another way to create a UCE—Dole repackaged lettuce. Instead of forcing consumers to purchase heads of lettuce at their supermarket, Dole precut and pre-washed the lettuce, then sealed it in convenient packages. For the busy consumer, this meant an enormous savings in time. For Dole, it meant enhanced revenues and profit, as customers would pay more for a product that was more convenient—a "salad UCE."

Another method to create a UCE by shaking things up is to change the cast. In show business, when a television pilot isn't quite working, the programming executives will often suggest the producers recast some of the actors. With a different take on the role, sometimes this recasting enables a program to become a success. Imagine if *All in the Family* had stayed with producer Norman Lear's original choice for Archie Bunker—Mickey Rooney. Instead, it was cast with Carroll O'Connor and became one of television's all-time classics. To enhance customer experiences and improve customer perceptions, perhaps you, too, need to "recast" your employees.

The first thing that probably comes to mind when you read this is to make changes in your staff. I will not deny that in many organizations this needs to take place. As my friend Mike Jackson, president of Agri Business Group (the leading consultants in the vast industry of agriculture), states, "If you hire a dud and spend a lot of money to train him or her, you end up with a trained dud." Many organizations have spent billions of dollars to train people who lack the skills necessary to execute their responsibilities. So yes, "recasting" could mean you need to change the people who work for you, but it could also mean that you just need to change the *perceptions* of the people who work for you. For instance, transform your salespeople into "advisors." While this may sound like mere semantics, as a customer I can tell you from experience that I place a higher value on a "docu ment

You want customers that are amazed, astounded, thrilled—and loyal for life! You want the kind of customers who refer you to their friends and can hardly wait to do business with you again. The way you create that kind of customer is to create and implement your Ultimate Customer Experience.

reproduction advisor" than I do on a "copy salesman." Do not forget our earlier point: behavior rewarded is behavior repeated. When you reward marketing professionals for advising clients rather than selling products, you get enhanced customer experiences and relationships. Advisors sell more than salespeople because customers are more open to recommendations from advisors than they are from salespeople. To use yet another example, I would prefer to deal with a "mortgage consultant" rather than a "home loan processor." Processing implies the customer is nothing more than a number. A consultant is there to assist, advise, and recommend the best alternative. Again, this serves to create a UCE.

An interesting part of this phenomenon is what psychologists call the Pygmalion Effect. This theory states that people live up (or down) to the expectations established for them. When you give an employee a title that carries the expectation of helpfulness and knowledge, he or she tends to live up to that expectation. So don't necessarily hire all new employees; instead, find ways to "recast" the employees you already have to create an enhanced customer experience.

Finally, if you are overwhelmed by all the changes and shake-ups required by the challenge of developing a high concept, story, and UCE, consider what former GE chairman and corporate superstar Jack Welch wrote in his book *Jack: Straight from the Gut*: "Only satisfied customers can give people job security. Not companies." Jack Welch understands, perhaps more than just about any other executive, the need to be an agent of change. I would simply replace the words "satisfied customers" in his quote with "emotionally connected customers."

You want customers that are amazed, astounded, thrilled—and loyal for life! You want the kind of customers who refer you to their friends and can hardly wait to do business with you again. The way you create that kind of customer is to create and implement your Ultimate Customer Experience.

ALL BUSINESS IS SHOW BUSINESS QUIZ

- Make a list of the expectations your high concept creates for—and promises it pledges to—your customers. Can your organization fulfill these expectations and promises?

- Make a list describing the emotional responses from your customers to your products and/or services. Is this list the same as a list of responses you *want* from your customers? How will you shape your UCE to deliver the appropriate emotions?

- When do your customers begin to experience your organization's products or services? What are your customers' "points of experience"—the encounters with receptionists, cashiers, assistants, sales professionals, managers, and so forth? Do each of these players realize their importance to the entire UCE?

- Write down how you will structure your UCE so that it becomes repeatable. How will you measure your unique UCE system so that you can fine-tune it?

- How do you reward customers for their business? How do you reward your employees for serving customers?

- What do your customers think the Ultimate Experience would look like?

Six

WHAT CUSTOMERS REALLY WANT

ecurity was high and everyone scheduled to be on an airplane that
day was tense. One of those things about life in America that we had
all taken for granted—safe, easy air travel—was being impacted by the
tragic events of September 11, 2001. Air service had returned, but trav-
elers were staying away in droves.

I had arrived at the airport two hours before my flight, expecting
to take a long time at the ticket line, the metal detector, and baggage
scanner. I was in for a surprise—the airport was like a ghost town. Less
than ten minutes after I walked into the terminal, I was finished at the
ticket counter, past the security checkpoint, and back at my gate for a
flight that still was a couple hours away from departure. For the first
time in all the years I had been a frequent flyer, everyone—passengers
and crew—viewed one another a little differently. Airline employees
understood more than ever before that their jobs depended on their
customers.

With only eight people on my flight that evening out of New York
City's LaGuardia, the United flight attendant struck up a conversation
as he tried his hardest to make an anxious situation return to normal
for his passengers and himself. "So what do you do that requires you
to be on an airplane today?" he asked me.

When I told him about my speeches and this book, his response was interesting—and on-target. "Sometimes I wonder," he said, "if managers who aren't out here on the front lines with customers really understand. Sure, passengers want things quickly, and they don't want to pay extra. But what they really, really want is to feel that someone with the airlines cares about how their trip is going. They want to feel we really do want to make it better."

In an issue of *Successful Meetings* magazine a while back, an article discussed the problems that planners and attendees of meetings were having with the airlines. A representative of one of my favorite airlines, United, was quoted as saying a very unfortunate thing. She said, in essence, that customers just have "no idea how difficult" it is to operate an airline.

Let's say I was booked to give a speech at a very important meeting for the top management team of United Airlines. In this hypo-

> **Customers seek a personal, emotional connection. As speaker and author Joe Calloway recently said, "My favorite restaurant is the one where they know my name!"**

thetical situation, my presentation runs an hour over its allotted time frame. I accidentally call "United" by the name of another airline. My jokes are offensive and crude. Then, when I'm confronted by angry executives after the program, I say to them, "Wait a minute. I give over a hundred speeches a year and write books as well. I have to travel all over the country and I am not home nearly as much as I would like to be. I have to learn about every company I work with and sometimes I just get tired. *You just have no idea how difficult it is* to be a speaker and author."

At that point, do you suppose the expression on their faces will soften, and they will pat me on the back as they say, "You know, you're right. It must be tough. We apologize. Here's double the amount of your fee to make it up to you"?

Not likely! Instead, they will say, "Too bad. Your job was to come here and give an excellent presentation no matter what the obstacles were. If you can't do it, don't take the job."

Don't get me wrong, my clients are nice people—but they basically don't care about anything other than my performance in front of their group. I am the same way when I am the customer. I do not care if United is on time for 99 percent of their other flights . . . just don't be late for *mine.*

The United flight attendant created a satisfying experience for me on that flight simply by talking with me in the manner that he did. He was a real pro. He didn't talk about how "tough it was" for him to do his job. The flight attendant proved by his actions that he knew what matters in customer relationships.

Customers seek a personal, emotional connection. As speaker and author Joe Calloway recently said in a presentation to the American Staffing Association, "My favorite restaurant is—*the one where they know my name!*"

WHAT CUSTOMERS WANT

When we try to create what customers really want, we need to keep the *customer's* point of view in mind through all the steps we take. What *you* think really does not matter to the customer. Customers are only interested in your perspective when they feel it matches theirs. The hard, cold, cruel fact is that customers do not really care how difficult it is for you to create the ultimate experience for them.

Customers want to know you have the ability to provide what they need in the way they need it. Seven performance "abilities" encompass what customers really want:

1. Access-ability
2. Approach-ability
3. Rely-ability
4. Customize-ability
5. Upgrade-ability/Dispose-ability
6. Enjoy-ability
7. Remark-ability

If you are the kind of manager the flight attendant was talking about—the one who does not know what it is like on the front line and is, therefore, disconnected from truly knowing what customers want—you're in deep trouble. If you are a business owner that focuses more on your product than knowing your customers' names, the clock is ticking down. I don't mean these as idle threats; I really believe you have a wake-up call coming. I also believe many businesses are in such a deep sleep that they may only arouse after it is too late to save their organizations.

Customers want to know you have the "ability" to provide what they need in the way they need it. Seven performance "abilities" encompass what customers really want: Access-ability, Approach-ability, Rely-ability, Customize-ability, Upgrade-ability/Dispose-ability, Enjoy-ability, and Rely-ability.

Remember our earlier definition of business: *The purpose of any business is to profitably create emotional connections that are so satisfying to customers and employees that loyalty is assured.* These seven "abilities" will be touchstones to help you make this true for your customers (and in the next chapter, for your employees).

ACCESS-ABILITY

Customers want to know that they can easily gain access to your organization so that they can do business with you. Not all that long ago having an 800 number was a unique differentiation in the marketplace. Now it is just part of the price of doing business. Unfortunately, many customers have to wait for an unbelievably long time before being able to talk to someone. When time is a precious commodity, making someone wait is detrimental to business. Access-ability is not just having an 800 number, or e-mail address, so customers can contact you. Access-ability is making it easy for your customers to get in touch with you without a long wait or complicated automated phone system.

When I jokingly told a woman with a prominent mobile telephone company that I wasn't going to start my speech until I got a person on the line after calling her company's 800 number, I thought she was going to have a heart attack. "Oh, no!" she exclaimed. "You can't do that with us. Your speech is only an hour long!" This story is sad, but true.

These are four main barriers that companies often establish that hinder access-ability:

1. Pinpoint responsibility

2. Technological extremism

3. Technological phobia

4. Understaffing

PINPOINT RESPONSIBILITY

If a company fails to make absolutely clear that *everyone's* job is the customer, then customers will make it clear by going someplace else. Pinpoint responsibility is when employees strictly follow the responsibilities as narrowly defined by their job description. When employees aren't proactive in helping customers, they can easily get caught in the middle of a transferring war between departments. Customers should *never* be told to "call back later" or "try another number." One specialist should help them access another to get the problem resolved. Everyone in your organization needs to view himself or herself as a "customer concierge."

Recently, I called AT&T Wireless for an answer to a question and accidentally dialed the number for residential customer service. I asked the customer service representative who answered if she could give me the number I should have called. "Hold just a moment," she said. A few seconds later, she returned and said, "Mr. McKain, I have Jane with AT&T Wireless Services now on the line with us. She can handle your question. Is there anything else I can do for you before I let you two talk?" Wow! That's what this customer wanted. That's "access-ability"!

TECHNOLOGICAL EXTREMISM

Technology has made a number of wonderful advancements possible in customer access. Voice mail systems, for example, are a great way to direct people to the right departments, but there should always be a way to escape the automated prison. Customers don't like being trapped in "voice mail jail," having a question and not being able to talk to a real person, being told to "leave a message and someone will get back to you."

I was calling a company recently and none of the options given on voice mail was what I was really looking for. I wasn't certain if my problem was a billing situation or a service outage. When I pressed *0*, the system reprimanded me by saying, "Zero is not a valid option." How about letting me press the *C* key for confused?

TECHNOLOGICAL PHOBIA

Some organizations, however, err on the side of having no technology, and won't work in today's marketplace. If you refuse to get e-mail because you're afraid of computers, you're going to miss out on a whole segment of the population that is doing more and more business online, whether it's promotions, invoicing, or ordering.

When I first moved to California, I went to a nearby dry cleaner—and found the people were friendly, but they still used handwritten tickets and a card file box for filing. If you picked up your cleaning anytime between five and six in the afternoon, you were going to wait in line as they rifled through the card box to find your clothes. They did a great job at cleaning but a horrible job using technology to provide service. I switched to another cleaners that is just as friendly and has a highly sophisticated computer system. They gave me a bag that has a bar code on it so I can just stuff it with dirty clothes and leave it anytime, even after hours in a drop box in front of their store.

The key here, obviously, is balance. Don't become so resistant to technology that you inadvertently put up roadblocks to customer access.

UNDERSTAFFING

When there are challenges in the economy, the initial cuts many organizations make are to the front-line employees. Banks cut back on tellers, supermarkets cut back on cashiers, and airlines lay off ticket counter agents. And customers end up standing in longer and longer lines.

When standing in a long line at a grocery store I asked a manager why the lines were so long. He told me that business was down, and they were having to make do with a smaller staff. Well, their business went down a little more because I never went back. Who wants to wait in a long line?

You can "save" your organization right into extinction! You can cut staff and economize on budgets . . . right up to the point that customers get fed up and go elsewhere, exacerbating the very problem you were trying to solve. Please don't think I am being naïve; in our companies with Obsidian Enterprises, we are sensitive to the fact that changing needs for employment require that tough decisions be made. But you don't do so in a manner that creates access difficulties for your customer. If you don't have enough staff to take care of the people trying to do business with you, you fail to create positive emotional connections that are so satisfying to customers and employees that loyalty is assured.

APPROACH-ABILITY

Customers will shy away from products and services they find intimidating. They want products that are easy to use, stores and locations that are comfortable, and services that are easy to understand; in short, they want companies to be "approachable."

Approach-ability is what customers want *after* they find accessability. After they have accessed an organization, customers should feel comfortable dealing with the company. It means that doing business with you is not intimidating and that your product is easy to use for the audience you are targeting.

In the earlier AT&T Wireless example, the manner in which the customer service representative handled the situation was perfect from the "access-ability" point of view. After I was handed off to the proper CSR, it then became *her* job to provide "approach-ability" as well. In other words, once the access to the right agent was obtained in a timely and seamless manner, the *next* thing I wanted as a customer was to be treated in a friendly, kind, and caring manner that demonstrated AT&T Wireless's concern for my business.

In the early days of personal computing, Macintosh's success was clearly driven by its "approachability." It was easy to understand and easy to use. The release of Windows 95 made computing with non-Macintosh machines infinitely more approachable than previous system software from Microsoft. Because you had to purchase a Macintosh computer made by Apple to use the Macintosh system software, PC's running Windows were now more *accessible*. I believe that part of why Windows—and therefore, Microsoft—became the dominant force in computing is because it is both more accessible and approachable than its competition.

One of my favorite places to stay is the Four Seasons Aviara Resort near San Diego. The hotel is so superb, in fact, that I purchased an interval ownership condominium there. (They used to call them "time shares.") While some might feel a little intimidated by the high quality of the surroundings, the warmth of the staff at Four Seasons Aviara would put anyone "at home." They understand the importance of "approach-ability." While the resort is upscale, there isn't the feeling of haughtiness or arrogance that many properties of this distinction attempt to exude. How do they do it?

They accomplish approach-ability by building what I call a "reservoir of goodwill." They build these reserves of good feelings by following these four steps:

1. Giving more personal contact
2. Doing the little things
3. Getting senior management involved
4. Dialoguing with the customers

Your organization can use these steps to build your own deep reservoir of goodwill.

GIVING MORE PERSONAL CONTACT

At Four Seasons Aviara, believe it or not, the staff memorizes your name! Heading out the front door with my golf clubs, the bellman—

to my utter astonishment—smiled and said, "Hit 'em straight today, Mr. McKain!" They even use technology to personalize the experience. When I get out of my car at check-in and give the bellman my name, he surreptitiously radioed my name to the front desk. When they pull me up on the database, they see all of my information, and by the time I reach the front desk, the clerk is saying, "Great to have you back, Mr. McKain! How was your drive down from Westlake Village?" If they know my name, they have made a personal contact greater than any I receive at competing hotels.

DOING THE LITTLE THINGS

Four Seasons Aviara does so many little things right, it's difficult to know where to start. The sheets, for example, have a slightly higher thread count than those found at most hotels, so the bed is a little more like home. In the bar, they don't provide the normal peanuts or pretzels but expensive mixed nuts. When you are packed up and ready to pull away from the hotel, the bellman hands you bottles of cold water to enjoy on your drive home.

Doing so many little things right builds into a *big* thing—a UCE! It shows they care enough to think of what the customer needs, from the customer's perspective. By doing the little things, they create the ultimate feeling of approachability—you aren't a customer; you are a *guest*.

GETTING SENIOR MANAGEMENT INVOLVED

I had arrived for a massage at the hotel health club, only to find that the therapist with whom I had an appointment had to leave early because of illness. Naturally, I understood; that can happen to anyone, anytime. Unfortunately, I wasn't going to be able to reschedule, because I had to check out early the next morning.

When I returned to my room, the phone was ringing. "Mr. McKain," the general manager said, "I am so sorry we weren't able to fulfill the appointment you had made today." It wasn't a big deal. It certainly was not important enough for the hotel's general manager to spend time being concerned about it, but I sure was impressed that he did. He even offered me a free bottle of wine with dinner that night.

The involvement of senior management is a powerful tool to display "approach-ability." If the general manager cares about my massage, what does that say about everything else at the hotel?

DIALOGUING WITH THE CUSTOMERS

After my first stay, I received a letter from Four Seasons Aviara asking me to indicate my preferences so they could serve me better. What kind of bottled water did I like? What was my favorite wine? What sports did I enjoy? My wife happens to love Evian, while I don't. In fact, I like just about every other kind of water (including tap) better than Evian. I jokingly made a note of that on the card. The next time we checked into the hotel, there in the room were two complimentary bottles of water—one Evian, one not.

Immediately after almost every visit to Four Seasons Aviara, I get either a phone call or a letter thanking me for my visit and—even more important—asking for what they could do to improve the experience. In our personal lives, we usually ask only those who we feel are important, perceptive, or qualified to give us advice. Therefore, the mere asking for information and advice creates higher feelings of approach-ability.

RELY-ABILITY

When I had the opportunity to interview film superstar Tom Hanks, I was amazed by one of his answers. When I asked him what were the main qualities that had contributed to his enormous success, Hanks replied, "I am not successful." Naturally, I responded that I thought he was being unnecessarily modest. He was emphatic in his response. He said, "Oh, don't get me wrong. If you are making a movie, you probably want to consider having me appear in it. I understand how the business works, and I am a hot commodity right now. However, I believe that true success is found in giving reliable, consistent, excellent performances over an extended period of time. Gregory Peck, James Stewart, John Wayne—that's success. I believe the jury is still out on me. The degree of my success is something that will be answered a few years down the road."

Tom Hanks realizes that in show business, as in any business, much of success is based on the reliability of the product and performer.

Rely-ability has a threefold meaning:

1. Consistency
2. Uniformity
3. Quality

CONSISTENCY

Show business has learned the value of consistency. The kiss of death for a new television show is usually when it has its time slot switched several times. A while ago, NBC had a low-rated program that it moved a couple of times. The result was that its small audience couldn't find it because it wasn't reliably broadcast—same time, same channel—every week. When NBC finally left it on Thursday nights, the program that was once at the bottom of the ratings soared to the top. Its name was *Cheers.*

If you or your organization's performance is erratic, then it is unreliable and therefore, something customers want to avoid. Few customers are willing to take a chance on you if they aren't pretty certain you are going to be able to come through for them.

UNIFORMITY

Part of McDonald's secret is their reliability. They have dependable and consistent performance, wherever you buy the product. In other words, a Big Mac is a Big Mac, whether it is purchased in Portland, Oregon, or Portland, Maine.

In these changing times, customers still want something on which they can depend. Even though the demands of customers are changing, they want a uniform performance from *you*. After I have experienced the sheets at the Four Seasons, I don't want to check in the next time and find that the beds are covered with the cheapest linens they could find from a discount store! This aspect of "reliability" means that after I have accessed your business and feel it is approachable, I want to know I can have that experience again.

QUALITY

If you make a promise, either directly to customers or through your advertising, they had better be able to rely on your commitment. An organization that cannot deliver on its commitments will not succeed in the long term. You must have a quality product or service—and, perhaps even more important, you must be an organization that exudes a sense of quality and integrity.

We all have heard of those organizations that promise a "quick fix" or "instant riches." Usually, these are the organizations that are unable to sustain any kind of profitability over the long haul. I have a dark side that delights just a bit when I read that another "no money down" or "get rich quick" infomercial guru has filed for bankruptcy. If you cannot deliver what you promise, then you get what you deserve. If you lack integrity, then you also lack quality. Some, however, who merchandise their goods through infomercials are ethical and adhere to a high quality standard. I was a participant in one such project. Part of what we discovered was that many were encouraging us to inflate our claims to stimulate sales. We refused. If you really want to make an enduring emotional connection with your customers, you cannot promise more than you can deliver.

Quality is found in an absolute commitment to a reliable, consistent standard. One of my wife's friends was about to have her home photographed for the cover article of a national magazine. My wife wanted to send her a bouquet of fresh flowers for the occasion. She placed her order with Hallmark Flowers several days in advance to guarantee that the flowers would be delivered in plenty of time for the photo shoot. Unfortunately, Hallmark's computers went down, and the order wasn't delivered on time. To their credit, Hallmark called my wife before she found out that the delivery had not happened as scheduled. They apologized profusely and delivered the flowers the following morning. Then, they credited my wife's charge card for the entire amount of the order! "You're not going to pay a penny for this," they told her. "You shouldn't be charged if we don't do what we say we'll do."

Certainly, my wife was disappointed that the flowers were not delivered on time. However, by showing their total commitment to quality, Hallmark will get another chance to deliver flowers for my wife.

Your customers have to be able to rely on what you make, what you do—and on *you*.

CUSTOMIZE-ABILITY

Since "ALL Business Is Show Business"—and show business is about making emotional connections—it stands to reason that we feel a greater connection with something that has been customized for us. When a product is customized, we tend to feel a greater sense of ownership and pride. The automobile is a great example here. When we can buy a car with the color and options we select, we feel it has become "our" car, not one that the manufacturer has assembled and we happened to purchase. We tend to take pride in it, because it has the features we want, in the look we've chosen to specifically fit our tastes.

Customizing a product or service promotes approach-ability, as mentioned earlier with the Four Seasons Aviara. If you are involved in the creation of the product or service, it is easier to understand and use the product or service. This provides the highest degree of emotional connection with your customer. When I feel as if the product has been built just for me, I have an amazing emotional tie to it.

Dell Computers is simply amazing when it comes to "mass customization" for customers. Call their toll-free number—or, as more people are doing every day, contact their site on the Internet—and you can choose the processor speed, hard drive size, memory configuration, and additional peripherals you want. They will custom-build the machine for you—often at a price lower than their competitors— and ship it directly to your home or office. This has enabled what was once a tiny start-up business to become a major player in one of the nation's most competitive businesses.

The first steps to "customize-ability" are simply asking these three questions:

- *What is my product?* If you're manufacturing cars, you aren't going to say to customers, "Want a lawn mower? Sure, we'll customize it and make it!" You don't do that. Define—at the most basic level—what the product is. Cars? Hamburgers? Hairstyles? Computers? What is it?

- *What are the variables?* Make a list of *all* the options possible. This may be an extremely long list. (If it isn't, maybe you aren't offering enough options!) Color? What goes on it or in it? Wash and blow dry . . . or not? Processor speed and hard drive size? Write it all down!

- *How can I put more decisions in the hands of customers?* Are there systems that will get this done for you? Can you hook an order form on the web to your manufacturing plant? Is there a checklist for customers to fill out when they enter your business?

Even show business is working in the area of customize-ability. Everything from pay-per-view movies to interactive games indicates that the entertainment business is moving toward the *audience* designing the product they want. Some of the most rapid areas of growth for the future in show business will come from the audience being able to custom design their viewing schedule for television, as witnessed by the growth of products like "TiVo." TiVo digitally records the shows you select and essentially allows you to program your television. You create your own personal "network." That's customizability—and it is the future.

UPGRADE-ABILITY/DISPOSE-ABILITY

While these two at first seem to be separate concepts, I am putting "upgrade-ability" and "dispose-ability" together, because what customers really want is one or the other.

Upgrade-ability means we are able to experience the maximum amount of benefit possible from your product and service—even as times and situations change—because we are given options to modify the product or service so that it keeps pace with changes in technology or other advances.

As consumers, we fear obsolescence. We have all probably had the experience of purchasing what seemed to be a "state-of-the-art" computer, only to find that in a few short weeks there was another faster and cheaper model. In a short period of time, our major investment was headed for the scrap pile. Many of us in small business proclaimed we were going to wait for future advancements and not get burned again. It still bothers me that the very expensive laser printer I purchased many years ago is now qualified to be nothing more than a door stop.

One of the world's most visionary companies, Microsoft, makes certain you know their products are always upgradeable. In fact, they combine many of the "abilities" we are discussing here and wrap them in their upgrade policy. For example, a Microsoft upgrade is easily accessed; you can upgrade your product from Microsoft by making a purchase from your local computer store, a mail order catalog, or even from the Microsoft web site.

Because of our fear of obsolescence, we will now pay more for products we can upgrade. Given the choice between a product that may be out of date in an unknown period of time (but probably short, given today's rate of change) versus one that will be upgradeable, the customer will often make the choice to go with the surer, upgradeable bet. The exception to this is when a product is easily *disposable*.

The story has often been told about the young entrepreneur who sought counsel from the wise businessman. "The way to riches," the philosopher said, "is to make a product that will be used repeatedly. But make it cheap enough that it can be disposed of so customers will want to purchase more."

That young entrepreneur took the advice to heart. This is how King Gillette founded his disposable razor company. Until that time, razors were purchased and sharpened on a strap. By saving his customers the time and effort of sharpening their razors and by making them cheap enough so that people felt free to throw them away and buy more, Gillette created an industry.

The worst place, however, for any product or service is somewhere in limbo between upgradeable and disposable. If your product or service is in danger of becoming obsolete, yet it's too expensive to throw away, you are in this purgatory. It is a scary place for customers . . . and can become death to an organization that attempts to sustain that position over any extended period of time.

ENJOY-ABILITY

The enjoyment factor must be woven into the fabric of your product or service so seamlessly that it becomes an intricate part of what you have to offer. For example, Ruth's Chris Steak House makes certain that you hear the steak sizzling when it is delivered to your table. The presentation is not *of* the product—the presentation *is* the product! The sizzle, the steak, and the server are all amalgamated in customers' minds and emotions into a meaningful whole—an experience.

How do you put enjoy-ability into your business? First, *you* have to enjoy the experience of serving your customers. The great performers of all time have fun—because they have passion and love for their craft. That doesn't mean they take it lightly. In the same way, the great athletes of all time are alike in one aspect: they all have fun on their respective fields of play, yet they all take their games seriously. If you don't truly enjoy doing what you're doing, you won't be able to get anyone else to be enthused about it, either. You have to transmit that sense of fun to your employees as well—so they deliver it to customers.

What "show biz" kinds of things can you add to your customer's experiences? A television and coffee pot in the waiting room? Cookies from Mrs. Fields? When you check in the Mirage hotel in Las Vegas, you sometimes encounter long lines. However, the enormous aquarium behind the front desk keeps you occupied; watching the fish makes your wait more enjoyable. Ask *your* customers what would make the experience more enjoyable for them. McDonald's built an empire based on kids taking parents to see a clown and eating some food while they were there.

But what if your business is a highly scientific one, for example a company that makes high-precision technical instruments? Or how about if you own and operate a funeral home? Customers of these products and services are not after an "enjoyable experience"—or are they? Just as all show-business products obviously do not revolve around humor, neither is it mandatory for the show-business organization to define an *enjoyable* experience as being one that is solely *fun*. As mentioned earlier, *Schindler's List* was not supposed to be amusing. It was, however, a very powerful emotional experience. The same is true if you run a funeral home or other business in which *fun* is not the appropriate response. A recent documentary that aired on HBO about the AIDS crisis was certainly not intended to create the same audience experience as the latest episode of *Frasier*. However, it *was* highly informative in terms of defining and explaining the latest scientific advances against this deadly disease and putting human faces on the statistics.

The word "enjoyable" means easy, hassle-free, and empathetic. To create an enjoyable experience, you do not have to create one that provokes laughter. What you must do, however, is create one that customers want to repeat.

REMARK-ABILITY

Today's customer not only wants but *demands* that a business, product, or service is remarkable. In other words, there must be something about you, your products, your services, and the experience you create for the customer that is unique. The only way to be unique is to differentiate your product or service in the minds of your customers. For your product or service to be remarkable, it must not only be unique, but it must also exhibit all the other "abilities" mentioned. If your business is not *remarkable*, you are doomed to mediocrity.

I mentioned that over 70 percent of customers say they would go someplace else if it were more "entertaining" to do business there. One reason this statistic is valid is because customers do not notice a significant divergence in the products and services they are offered from one supplier to the other.

When a company finds a unique way to present itself to its customers, the response is remarkable. For example, let's use Southwest Airlines again. The way it presents the preflight safety instructions in a manner that is entertaining and enjoyable is a point of differentiation. This "remark-ability" is part of the reason why Southwest Airlines enjoys such high praise from its customers—and is rewarded by its customers with repeat business, even though it provides little of the perks assumed to be the definition of "service."

Tom Peters, one of the top "business gurus" in the country, describes this phenomenon in his book *The Pursuit of WOW!* As Peters studied exceptional businesses, he determined that as times were changing so was the standard desired by customers. In other words, no longer were they searching for excellence; now they were pursuing something that would make them go, "Wow!" They want to experience a product or service that does more than simply satisfy them; they want to be amazed.

Before I moved to California, I was shopping in Indianapolis for a big-screen television. I shopped at three different stores and eventually bought the same television for thirty dollars more at H. H. Gregg, a regional appliance chain, than I could have spent at Best Buy or Circuit

City. The reason I didn't hesitate to pay a little more was because they have *same-day* delivery. The other stores didn't get the sale for one main reason. Even though I was spending over two thousand dollars, I wanted it *now*. H. H. Gregg had knowledgeable salespeople, and they (like their competition) were easy to access and approachable once I got there. However, Gregg's differentiation in delivery was enough to make me view them as "remarkable." And that made the sale. *Excellence* would mean getting the big-screen television delivered without a scratch, set up properly, at the appointed time. *Wow* means you buy it in the store and are watching it in your own home that same day.

As I lecture around the country, one of the things I am constantly asked is how to deal with the issue of a competitor having a lower price. If the customer sees no differentiation in terms of the product or service between you and your competitor, the customer has no reason to choose anything *other* than the lower priced product. Unless you can describe your unmatched advantages to your customers in a persuasive manner, the customer will naturally buy the cheaper alternative. However, when you are perceived as remarkable, customers are willing to invest more money to purchase what you have to offer. If you don't believe this, then please explain why we are standing in line to buy coffee at three dollars a cup from Starbucks. It is not so much that Starbucks coffee is better than their competition. Rather, what is important is that their customers *believe* it is, and what's more, they see Starbucks as a "hip" neighborhood gathering place. It is these perceptions of remark-ability that convinces you to pay more and encourages you to return frequently.

WHAT YOU DO IS WHAT COUNTS

Visionary organizations are able to see the future of their products and services. They are also able to see how the "abilities" we've just discussed will help them meet the needs, wants, and demands of today's— and tomorrow's—customers.

So, perhaps the question I should be asking is this one: How important are customers to you individually and organizationally? You should seriously consider your answer. After all, if my dry cleaner tells me that customers are important, then they had better prove that by providing the seven "abilities" I want. The same is true with my supermarket, airline, auto dealer, and everything else.

If you want to be an author, you take the time and you write a book. You put the seat of your pants in the seat of the chair, and you do it. If you don't take the time to do it, then you aren't an author. If you want to be a good parent, you spend time with your kids. You do things with them, encourage them, and take an active role in their lives. If you are just a spectator in their growth rather than a participant, being a mom or dad evidently isn't that important to you.

What are you willing to do to deliver the seven "abilities" customers want?

Your answer to this question is important if you want your business to survive in the twenty-first century.

ALL BUSINESS IS SHOW BUSINESS QUIZ

- How easy is it for customers to contact your organization? How easy is it to get answers they need?

- Do your customers feel comfortable doing business with you? How can you employ the four steps listed on page 136 to obtain a "reservoir of goodwill"?

- Are you producing quality products and services upon which people can rely? Does your organization radiate quality so that customers rely on what you say and do?

- Do you make your products and services fit the unique needs and desires of your customers?

- Are your products upgradable? If not, are they priced in a manner that allows them to be disposable?

- How can you engineer enjoyment for your customers into all the products you sell and all the services you provide?

- Is it easy for your customer to distinguish what makes you different and unique? Do your products and services "wow!" your customers? How?

~

SEVEN

WHAT EMPLOYEES REALLY WANT

At a conference in Ft. Lauderdale, I heard one of the other speakers on the program, Mel Kleinman, propose this thought-provoking question to the audience: "Do customers come first?"

Of course we have all had these clichés drummed into our heads: "The customer is *always* right!" "Customers *always* come first!" So the group responded as we have all been trained: *"Yes!"*

To which Kleinman countered, *"No!* Employees should come first! When employees come first," he continued, *"they* will put customers first! And isn't that *really* what you and your organization want?"

Of course. This is what we call the "blinding flash of the obvious." If we turn again to show business, we'll see this same principle in action.

One of the most successful creations in the history of entertainment is the character of Indiana Jones. The three movies about the action-oriented archeologist are among the highest grossing films of all time. Indiana Jones movies are classics, and if they make a fourth film, you and I will probably be there to see it.

So here is a question for you: The character of Indiana Jones is, in reality, an intellectual property owned by its creators, George Lucas and Steven Spielberg. But when I mentioned "Indiana Jones" in the first sentence of this story, did you think of Lucas and Spielberg?

Obviously not. You thought of Harrison Ford.

No matter what your favorite scene is—from *Raiders of the Lost Ark* through the sequels—when you think of Indiana Jones you envision the *character*: Harrison Ford wearing the hat, holding the whip, a day's growth (or more) of beard on his chin, looking a little sweaty, and seeking adventure. I'll bet that right now you can hear in your head the theme music by composer John Williams!

The point is this: Lucas and Spielberg *own* Indiana Jones; Harrison Ford *is* Indiana Jones!

And employees *are* the company. In the audience's mind, the employee is the business, whether that employee is Harrison Ford or your sales rep in Dubuque. You can own your company, you can manage your division—but your employees *are* the company or division. Their experience will be the genesis of the experience they create for the customer.

I know some of you reading this book right now are saying to yourselves, "Wait a minute. I pay people to be professionals. They are supposed to show up, hit the mark, and do their jobs. Their emotional relationship with the job is their choice, not mine." If this is your way of thinking, you had better think again. You had better start creating emotional connections that build employee loyalty. *You can't afford to do otherwise!*

You have probably seen the statistics that seem to constantly appear in the business press on the costs of obtaining new customers. You may be surprised, however, how much it costs your organization when an *employee* leaves. The consulting firm Kepner-Tregoe of Princeton, New Jersey, attempted to measure the turnover costs at fifteen corporations. All the organizations surveyed were astonished at the results. When you include such items as severance pay and exit interviews, replacement hiring costs and lost productivity while the new hire was learning the job, a fast-food chain discovered that when a store lost a manager, the cost to the company was $21,931. One manufacturer was amazed to find that the loss of a salaried journeyman machinist had cost their company $102,796. To fire an automaker's human resource manager cost the organization a whopping $133,803. According to consultant Quinn Spitzer of Kepner-Tregoe, the study revealed astounding bottom-line losses in every industry. He found the connection between employee loyalty and profits "unassailable."

An article in the *Washington Times* quotes Steve Walker, president of Walker Information, a globally respected management consulting firm: "There is no doubt that there is a connection between an employee's level of commitment to a company and his or her job performance. If businesses want to increase employee productivity and bottom-line results, they need to address this issue quickly."

Loyal employees create loyal customers! When you establish a remarkable emotional connection between the organization and the employees, they create amazing emotional connections with customers.

WHAT EMPLOYEES WANT

A study by the Hudson Institute, a Washington, D.C.- and Indianapolis-based public policy research group, shows us that organizations are facing a massive challenge. According to their study, only 51 percent of employees would recommend their organizations as a good place to work. The study of 2,000 full- and part-time employees in the United States also revealed that only 45 percent feel a strong personal attachment to their organization or believe their organization even *deserves* their loyalty. Richard W. Judy, a researcher at the Hudson Institute, states, "This study clearly points out that employers need to focus on building relationships with their workers so that these employees truly believe that they are a valued part of the team."

THE ULTIMATE EMPLOYEE EXPERIENCE

In other words, just as customers want the UCE—Ultimate Customer Experience—in today's business culture, employees are looking for a UEE—the Ultimate Employee Experience. Just like customers, employees have an amazing desire to be emotionally connected. Remember the definition of the purpose of business: *The purpose of any business is to profitably create emotional connections that are so satisfying to customers and employees that loyalty is assured.* Loyal employees create loyal customers! When you establish a remarkable emotional connection between the organization and the employees, *they* create amazing emotional connections with customers.

If you want to be a partner with your employees in developing an Ultimate Employee Experience, you should encourage the development of a personal high concept and deliver to your employees the promise made by your company's story. The personal high concept will give your employees a better perspective and purpose concerning their job, which in turn will improve their attitude and devotion. And when you tell your employees that they are valuable, you should also show them that they are valuable through your actions. This will create an emotional bond that will lead to loyalty.

To assist in developing a UEE, each employee should be encouraged to create a personal high concept. Just like the high concept for a business discussed earlier in this book, an employee's personal high concept will be a short, powerful, attention-grabbing statement that will define his or her special position in the company. When individual employees create a unique statement like the high concept, an amazing transformation happens—they feel more important! Remember the woman in payroll we discussed in an earlier chapter? Now that she no longer merely processes payroll but instead funds the dreams of hundreds, her entire perspective on her life has been transformed.

When a company fails to deliver on its promise to its employees, it doesn't matter how good the employees' high concepts are, their perspectives will dwindle. The employees will see that the company doesn't care, so why should they? They will either take their time, talent, and abilities elsewhere or they will act in a manner that will encourage your customers to seek another place to do business—or both!

Once again, Southwest Airlines does it right. (Notice a pattern here?) When air travel dramatically declined after the terrorist attack in New York City in September 2001, most airlines reduced employee numbers by the thousands. Southwest had a different approach. Because they have a commitment to deliver on their story to their employees as well as their customers, they went to their colleagues and basically said, "Look, these are challenging times. If you are willing to work one less day per week, we will keep everyone and there will be no layoffs." By demonstrating their loyalty to their employees,

Southwest Airlines charted a path of growth for their company while competitors had to retreat. I'm certain airline analysts would suggest— and perhaps rightly so—that much more is involved here. However, the bottom line is that while other companies keep working harder at the old plan and digging themselves into a deeper hole with employees and customers; Southwest has a different approach that *succeeds*.

Since your employees, like your customers, are people, too, it should not surprise you that your employees want similar things. This means that the basic "abilities" we discussed in the previous chapter will also make up the "abilities" that employees are looking for as well.

Now, let's take a look at what your employees want:

- Access-ability
- Approach-ability
- Rely-ability
- Customize-ability
- Upgrade-ability/Dispose-ability
- Enjoy-ability
- Remark-ability

ACCESS-ABILITY

The access-ability of an organization for an employee is their ability to make the employee feel part of a team, or a family. For employees, the accessible organization provides both a formal and informal structure that ensures the company listens—and *cares*. It is more than just policies and organizational structures that provide forums for feedback to enhance a feeling of interaction throughout the company, though. It is about management becoming so proactive that they hear the concerns of the employees before a complaint must be made. The caring has to be genuine and from the top. When an organization cares about its employees, the employees will, in turn, enjoy working harder for the "team."

Years ago, many companies had the policy that every employee had to spend some time in the field as a part of the sales force. The thinking behind this, of course, was that this approach would build a knowledgeable and experienced staff. In addition, the thinking went, this type of training early in a career would help a professional better understand the ramifications on the customers of organizational decisions. These shared experiences also went a long way toward building teamwork and a sense of ownership in the company.

Today, many employees have much more specific job responsibilities. The problem this creates within the employee framework is the breakdown of teamwork across divisional lines. The danger is that you can become an entire organization of professionals who have the "it's not my job" attitude.

Technology is another danger to the team. When employees have a problem and have to go to the company Intranet and fill out a form, the sense of personal caring vanishes. An employee of a mid-sized company once complained to me that in order to communicate with the human relations department, she had to fill out a form. She would then get a standard response that she was supposed to evaluate to see if it properly responded to her concern. If it did not, she was then asked to fill out another form and e-mail it to the HR department. After three tries, it was then corporate policy that she could pick up the phone and request a personal response. Naturally, this was an efficient procedure for the company. However, efficiency without emotional connections breeds a feeling of limited accessibility among your employees.

When technology and efficiency get in the way of the emotional connection between an organization and its employees, there is a breakdown of awareness by the management. Managers stop listening to their employees.

Once, after a seminar I was giving a vice president came up to me and asked, "Was there anything you picked up that we need to work on?"

"Well," I answered, "since you asked, I'll tell you. It was obvious from the one-on-one discussions I had with several employees that they feel the company needs to do a better job listening to them. They feel as though the access-ability you're asking them to provide to customers isn't there for them internally."

The VP's face turned pale. "I—I can't believe that," she stuttered. "For goodness sake, we have suggestion boxes and comment cards everywhere."

This is a perfect example of the differences between the system-based training we receive as professionals and the emotion-based responses we want as customers—and employees. Putting the systems into place—creating comment cards, suggestion boxes, and a special voice mailbox for ideas—can never take the place of a manager who listens. And a manager who listens to the employees and understands and responds to their needs is a manager who cares. This creates teamwork and access-ability.

APPROACH-ABILITY

For employees, approach-ability means this: Now that you have given me access, are you going to go to the next step and give me what I am looking for in a job?

My publisher, Larry Stone, and I were recently discussing this facet of employee relations. He told me that this aspect was really

> # Employee satisfaction is about creating stimulating mutual relationships among people who work for the same company!

driven home for him during a brainstorming session he was conducting for his employees. Larry asked them a very important question: "What do you want out of your jobs?"

In business, we are always telling employees what *we* want. We tell them when to show up; how to dress; when and where to travel; company policies and procedures; what is acceptable performance, sales quotas, or efficiency standards; and the list goes on and on. Companies that "get" what is happening in the culture today, however, are the ones who take the next step and ask that significant question Larry did: What do *employees* want from *us*?

Larry told me one person responded that she wanted three things: "Professional gratification. Social interaction. Money." Larry added, a note of surprise in his voice, "That was the order in which she put them!"

What Larry heard from his employee is similar to what you, too, will hear if you listen. Employee satisfaction is not just about flextime, job sharing, telecommuting, day care, and all the other innovations we hear so much about (although those are great things to provide). It *is* about initiating opportunities for your employees to find professional fulfillment. And it's about creating stimulating mutual relationships among people who have something in common—they work for the same company!

An organization's leaders can accomplish this in many ways, but here are three ways in particular through which they can accomplish this:

1. Recognition

2. Interdepartmental activities

3. Personal growth opportunities

RECOGNITION

Zapping through the channels on my television during a Sunday afternoon, I stopped for a moment on a soccer match being televised by a Spanish language network. Just as I happened on the channel, a player kicked the ball into the goal. Even though I neither speak Spanish nor understand all the rules of what the rest of the world calls "football," I could easily comprehend the significance of what had happened. The announcer shouted, "GOOOAAALLL!" The stadium's fans erupted in cheers. What I mainly noticed, however, was how the player that had scored the goal was mobbed by his teammates, and how he then practically took a victory lap around the field.

Just as in sports where we stand and cheer the winners after their victories, in business we must create methods to recognize our employees so they have a victory lap and a standing ovation; they need a chance to hear the roar of the crowd.

When professional speaker Charles Dygert addresses business groups, he will occasionally bring an audience member to the stage and ask him or her to stand front and center. Then he will turn to the crowd and have them give this person the biggest standing ovation in the history of the company. I have seen Dygert do this on several occasions, and I am always amazed by the results. Every single time, the person on stage starts by being embarrassed, but the next reaction is always the most astounding. One man broke down in tears. A woman did the same. Another man almost hyperventilated and had to leave the stage. One woman had so much emotion she started spinning in circles. Every person said it was the first time in their lives they had ever felt so appreciated.

It is important to show appreciation to your employees. Take some innovative steps to recognize good performances:

- Set specific goals for performance and give *everyone* who meets them something unique—an award, a day off, a gift certificate to take the family to dinner.

- Offer one paid personal day off with no questions asked each quarter when the desired results are achieved and maintained.

- Send a gift basket to the spouse of an employee who has put in extra time.

INTERDEPARTMENTAL ACTIVITIES

People who perform different tasks in your organization need a chance to talk and share with one another. Interdepartmental activities not only promote access-ability, they also build employee morale by encouraging teamwork.

In his book *Jack: Straight from the Gut,* former General Electric CEO Jack Welch recounts that some of the stimulus for the amazing growth at GE over the past two decades was generated by getting the people in one department to talk with people from another. It meant getting the division that made aircraft engines to think about not only selling the engine, but getting the buyer to finance it from GE Capital, as well.

Yet in many organizations, the sales staff has never had the chance to spend a day with an engineer to see how difficult it is to change the product. Few CEOs have ever spent time in the service department fixing the product the company manufactures.

If you design activities that foster communication between departments, this will enhance your ability to provide the social interaction—as well as stimulate the professional improvements—your employees' desire.

PERSONAL GROWTH OPPORTUNITIES

When employees know you are concerned about their personal growth, they will respond with professional productivity. According to a Canadian study conducted by N. Winter Consulting, employees want "challenging work, continuous learning, flexible work arrangements and better communication with their employers." But employers continue to focus on *compensation* as the foremost means to attract and retain. "Money is always an issue, but it is clearly not the only thing that matters to employees these days," said Nadine Winter, president of N. Winter Consulting. "Employees will sacrifice pay for opportunities to learn and grow." Remember the earlier example from my publisher's experience? Money was mentioned—but it was the third of the employee's three desires.

Marriott Hotels has devised a unique approach. They place a special emphasis on supporting the personal development of their employees, and their compensation system identifies the personal skills and abilities needed for a broad range of the jobs in their system. Marriott then designs a pay program that allows employees to take lateral assignments that could potentially develop their professional skills and broaden their experience within the organization without necessarily affecting their rate of pay.

By becoming an organization that exemplifies approach-ability, you provide the opportunities for professional gratification and social interaction that employees are craving. That means you will enhance emotional connections with employees so that they will become loyal—and create loyal customers.

RELY-ABILITY

For customers, we said that rely-ability meant consistent performance. The customer finds the reliable organization easy to recommend because it executes its responsibilities in a similar fashion every time.

Employees are asking for a similar quality from your organization. This may sound deceptively easy. It is not. With so many changes happening in our culture and so many demands placed on an organization, an organization may need to make changes within the corporate structure. These changes are well intended; in most cases, they are made to serve customers more effectively. However, these changes can also suggest to employees that the company is unreliable.

I have worked for many organizations that have told their employees that after one round of cutbacks there will be no more. Then, a few months later, the organization says, "Oops! We made a mistake. There is going to be another round of layoffs." Obviously these actions are understandable, but they also serve to warn the employees that what is said by management is totally unreliable. As the cliché goes, do you "say what you mean and mean what you say"? When you tell an employee something, is it reliable?

One Fortune 50 company for whom I have frequently worked is thrilled by their research and development division, but they are disappointed by their sales and service force. Meanwhile, to keep pace with their changing industry, the company has made so many organizational changes that some of their employees consider them to be unreliable. The R&D side is being treated in a very dependable and uplifting fashion; and they are responding with high performance. The sales and service staff, however, which has undergone several reorganizations and has not received the support they were promised, has a totally different view of the same management team.

One of the best managers with whom I have ever had the privilege of working is Bruce Johnston of Conseco Fund Group. One of the main reasons he is such a great manager is his consistency. He means what he says—and he proves it by his actions. Bruce is one of the most vibrant, charismatic, and personable leaders you will ever meet. At the same time, he sets standards for those he leads, measures their output, and responds in a consistent manner. This approach makes him totally reliable, and therefore he is the type of leader for whom people want to work.

Conseco Fund Group offered me an opportunity to give several speeches a year to their clients. Before my first appearance, Bruce told me that after every presentation the audience would be surveyed as to their satisfaction with my program. He told me that he would evaluate the sales figures generated by the clients after they heard my speech. This same approach was taken for every presenter. After several months, I was told that several speakers in the Conseco "Speakers Bureau" were not being retained. Their results were not up to Bruce's standards.

Later Bruce told me, "Scott, if your numbers and evaluations had not met the standards, it would not have impacted our friendship. It's just that you wouldn't be giving speeches for us anymore." I know he wasn't kidding.

One of Conseco Fund Group's sales representatives was recently fired by the organization. The person happened to be one of Bruce's personal favorites, and yet this person had not achieved the required sales and productivity goals. The rest of the team realized that if Bruce would terminate the employment of one of the people he liked best personally, they would *all* have to perform to keep their jobs. Bruce's consistency in his demands from *all* employees shows that he is reliable; in his book, politics are not as important as performance. That's an example of great management.

To prove that you are a reliable employer, you must apply your ethics and standards to all employees. Businesses of all sizes need to create a quality organization that is consistent in dealing with all their employees.

CUSTOMIZE-ABILITY

For customers, customize-ability is making the product or service fit their needs. For employees, it is making the job fit the experience they're seeking. The old-style method was to create the job description first, then find the employee to "plug" into that position. While we will never be able to completely get away from that approach, customize-ability means you are willing to modify a position to meet the strengths and desires of the individual employee. Naturally, you will need some give and take in this particular area. You are undoubtledly familiar with the phenomenon of the comic strip Dilbert—a humorous approach toward an organization preventing its employees from exercising their individual strengths. Most humorists tell you that the best humor is grounded in reality. If we examine the Dilbert phenomenon a little further, it clearly indicates that most employees feel their organization is trying to subvert—rather than enhance—their abilities to perform their jobs. As an avid reader of "Dilbert," I never get the impression the comic strip is anti-corporation. Dilbert is merely pro-customize-ability for employees.

Most employees feel their organization is trying to subvert— rather than enhance—their abilities to perform their jobs.

The way that most companies approach this issue seems to me to border on the insane. Organizations will customize software, products, services—just about everything except the job. Perhaps that is because companies, operating out of solely economic principles, fail to account for the emotional impact that "customize-ability" has on preserving the organization's intellectual capital. Maury Hanigan, founder of Hanigan Consulting Group in New York City, in the November 9, 1998 edition of *Fortune* notes that "If a $2,000 desktop computer disappears from an employee's desk, I guarantee there'll be an investigation, a whole to-do. But if a $100,000 executive with all kinds of client relationships gets poached by a competitor, there is no investigation. No one is called on the carpet for it."

If you value the intellectual capital of your organization, which is housed in the minds and emotions of your employees, then you will take the steps necessary to enhance that investment; you will provide "customize-ability" for your employees. Dave Ulrich, a professor at the University of Michigan Graduate School of Business, in the same *Fortune* article remarks that "Smart people want to know where they're headed, but they don't want to be told how to get there."

Why do organizations fail to provide customizable opportunities for their employees? Well, first of all, it goes against tradition. The old way of thinking in corporate America was that we would make the employee "peg" fit into the corporate "hole." Employee pegs that didn't fit into corporate holes were not to be tolerated. In those days it was an "employer's marketplace."

Times have changed. Now, visionary organizations must provide opportunities for their employees that are specific to each individual's needs, wants, and talents.

Notice, this does not contradict the "rely-ability" issue discussed earlier. The standards for performance should be consistent. The results should be measured and evaluated. However, we should allow employees the ability to customize their activities to get the results we want.

Organizations also fail to demonstrate "customize-ability," because, let's face it, customizing opportunities for employees is a difficult thing to do. It is much easier to write rules and regulations than it is to learn and manage individual talents. On the other hand, it's equally tough to build products—and companies do that anyway. It isn't easy to provide good customer service, either—yet many organizations manage to do that as well. Therefore, no excuse is a good one when it comes to the lack of "customize-ability" found at most companies.

"Customize-ability" may break with tradition and it may be difficult, but it is nevertheless essential in today's business world. Its two most important aspects are simply: the proper management attitude and a retention strategy more aggressive than your recruitment strategy.

MANAGEMENT ATTITUDE
The attitude of the employees is often a reflection of the attitude of management. You know this is true.

My friend Mark Mayfield was telling me about a group that hired him to speak at a company function not long ago. The organization was managed by a former military leader who had a reputation for trying to bring the "boot camp" philosophy to the corporate world. As Mark was driving to a pre-convention conference with the manager and his team at the company's home office, he received a call on his cell phone that his daughter had been involved in an automobile accident. Fortunately, she wasn't injured, but Mark was ten minutes late for the meeting because of his obvious need to make certain of her safety.

The manager told Mark upon his arrival that there was "never an excuse for being late." The more Mark tried to explain that his tardiness was not because of any disinterest or lack of professional organization or personal courtesy, the more the manager taunted him. Mark found that same insensitivity in every member of the management team. Interestingly, Mark's evaluation of the company was that it was not performing to its optimum level—because it was a culture of fear, not of relationships.

"Customize-ability" is really not just one "attitude"; instead, it is the expression of four traits that, when combined, present your employees with the kind of atmosphere that conveys a genuine concern for colleagues. These four traits are:

1. *Consideration.* Do you treat employees with civility and compassion? Do you consistently express your understanding of the challenges they face, personally and professionally?

2. *Sincerity.* Do you convey honesty and genuineness in your communication with employees? Are you earnest about the need to customize their jobs to enhance their performance and lifestyle?

3. *Openness.* Are you amenable to changing structure and policy to benefit people? Will you listen to the needs, wants,

and ideas of your employees? Do you truly believe that employees should be informed about what is going on in your organization?

4. *Responsiveness.* Do you react to employee requests in a timely fashion? Is their need to know an important factor in your decision-making process? Do you understand that their concerns are not hostile, but rather that they can enhance the organization?

RETENTION STRATEGY

"Why is it that only 54 percent of companies have retention strategies when 100 percent of them have recruiting strategies?" asks Sharon Jordan-Evans, coauthor of "Love 'Em or Lose 'Em: Getting Good People to Stay," in the January 15, 2001 issue of *InfoWorld*. "It's a fundamental disconnect," she says, "that guarantees companies will suffer from costly turnover."

But isn't this faulty strategy typical of the way most organization resources are focused? For some reason we spend more on getting the initial sale than we do on than serving current customers. We emphasize hiring good people rather than keeping the first-rate people already in our organization. "What attracts us and keeps us are different," Jordan-Evans says.

Don't forget: your top customers are your competition's primary targets, and by the same token, your best employees are also the ones your competitors covet. If you believe that customers are important to retain, why would you presume that employees aren't?

A critical first step in managers' training must be to educate them in strategies for keeping the best people. Employees don't leave companies; they leave their managers.

Harrison Ford returned to act in two "Indiana Jones" sequels for a primary reason: he loved working with Steven Spielberg. Sure, there was a lot of cash involved. But there wasn't enough money to get him to do something he really didn't want to do. He could have made millions filming another screenplay for another director, but he wanted the opportunity to have Spielberg direct him once more. You have to become the kind of manager that creates such powerful emotional connections that stars want to come back and give an award-winning performance for you again and again.

The second step needed in managers' training is to hold them accountable. Remember Dr. Michael LeBoeuf's GMP we discussed earlier: "Behavior rewarded is behavior repeated." If you hold managers accountable for employee retention and reward them for keeping employees, you will find managers will make retention a high priority. Make it hard on managers who time and again chase off key performers, or who insufficiently prepare new people for their responsibilities.

The question any organization must ask is, "Is it worth it?" When it comes to employee retention, the answer in these changing times is, undoubtedly, yes.

UPGRADE-ABILITY/DISPOSE-ABILITY

Here's an obvious job ability that employees desire. They either want the opportunity to continue to advance their careers internally (upgrade-ability), or the chance to learn a new and saleable skill in a relatively short period of time and move on (dispose-ability).

If employees feel they are able to upgrade their abilities—and be compensated for doing so by an organization—why would they want to leave? Part of the key to retaining your key people is to make certain they know they will have the opportunity to advance their skills, position, and compensation as a valuable member of your team.

On the other hand, some positions in many organizations do not avail themselves of a career track. Not all employees *want* upgradeable positions. For various reasons they simply may not want to spend their entire careers with you. This is not an insult to your organization; this is the reality of the marketplace. It is happening in many industries. For example, Department of Labor statistics report that only 56 percent of employees in banking and finance are assigned to conventional advancement schedules. The *St. Louis Post-Dispatch* reported recently that intentional part-time employment arrangements are increasing. According to the report, "A wide range of surveys note that a part-time work-life program is the most advantageous way for employers to reduce labor costs. Employees who choose these work arrangements obtain the flexibility necessary to satisfy their needs away from the workplace."

FedEx is a good example here. Naturally, those on the management track at FedEx are given the opportunity for upgradeable positions. However, many times the employees who load the planes at FedEx hubs such as Memphis and Indianapolis are people working a second job or are college students. They understand they are not on a lifelong career path with FedEx. However, FedEx gives them great advantages in this disposable position. They are allowed to travel for free in one of the jump seats in FedEx cargo planes. Even though they are part-time employees, they receive full medical and dental benefits. Many other amenities are given to these disposable positions as well. In this way, FedEx is able to maintain a significant part of its work force in part-time positions while attracting the kinds of workers they want to have with the company.

Organizations, however, must not think of disposable *positions* as being occupied by disposable *people*. One of the keys to the success of such organizations as FedEx and Wal-Mart is the way they deal with their part-time employees to make them understand that, even though the position may be considered disposable, the people who hold those positions are highly valuable to the organization.

ENJOY-ABILITY

My father always used to say, "There is a time for work and a time for play." I am not going to disagree with this statement—but I *am* going to suggest that the time to work and the time to play is the *same* time.

Ask yourself this basic question: Do your employees do a better job when they enjoy what they do or when they hate what they do? The answer is obvious. So why do so many organizations seem to make an effort to remove all the enjoyment from a job?

Several years ago when I was visiting automotive factories in Detroit, I was surprised to learn that one of the most challenging aspects in factory management was the prevention of employee sabotage. Apparently, workers on the assembly line were using their creative abilities to find ways to shut down the line. The only way these employees were able to derive significant enjoyment from their jobs was through their ability to screw things up for their employer. Thankfully, much has happened since the mid-1970s in this regard. Detroit has found that if you make the job more enjoyable for factory workers, not only does productivity go up but incidents of negative behavior go down.

At a November 1992 meeting of the American Heart Association, German researchers reported that 18 percent of employee heart attacks occur on a Monday morning, the beginning of the conventional workweek. The start of the week's work—10 percent of our time at work—produces almost 20 percent of the heart attacks! Some experts theorize that the stress involved with the workplace is responsible. According to a January 1994 *Parade* magazine article, the average American is in a bad mood 110 days each year! Clearly, there is a vital need to create more enjoy-ability in the workplace!

You can take many approaches to achieve enjoy-ability. A recent study conducted for Pepperidge Farm by Dorr Research Corporation invited diverse companies such as Eddie Bauer, Staples, General Electric, Gillette, Saatchi & Saatchi, and Campbell Soup to take part in a benchmark study to test the impact of Chocolate Chunk Classic Cookies in the workplace. The study produced these results: 88 percent of those surveyed agreed that their productivity and creativity were enhanced after enjoying the cookies; 84 percent agreed that the cookies helped them feel a little more comfortable at work; 77 percent reported the cookie breaks introduced an element of fun to the workplace; 58 percent agreed that the cookies put people they work with in a better mood; and 57 percent believed that having cookie breaks at their companies gave them a chance to talk with people they didn't usually have a chance to see.

I think this is a neat study. Frankly, however, I am less concerned about the impact of Pepperidge Farm Chocolate Chunk Classic Cookies in the workplace (hey, who could be *opposed* to cookies?) than I am impressed that the previously mentioned companies allowed the study to take place in their offices. Creating enjoy-ability at your organization might just start with cookies (and don't forget the milk). The important thing is to do *something!*

My friend Matt Weinstein, founder of Playfair Inc., and author of the book *Managing to Have Fun,* told *HR* magazine associate editor Phaedra Brotherton that he believes, "One of the key benefits to fun at work is the improved customer service that results from greater employee commitment to the organization. You get incredible corporate loyalty," he told the magazine. "Every company tells employees to deliver service with a smile. Internal customer service improves [by using humor], which translates into better external customer service."

Another benefit of fun at work is building or rekindling a team spirit. "It builds up a stronger sense of team," Weinstein says. "When people are laughing together, they're creating bonds between one another." He also states that laughter and fun "are a doorway, an entree into being more human with the people we work with."

Again, as we emphasized at the beginning of this book, "fun" does not mean "frivolous." You can enjoy what you do while taking it seriously at the same time. One of the most vital things any ordinary organization can do to become extraordinary is to find a way to script (or engineer, for you more technical types) enjoyment into the work process.

Employees who find their work situation enjoyable create the kind of enjoyable customer experiences we were discussing earlier. When employees have fun, this translates into customer enjoyment. Creating an enjoyable experience for your customers is truly serious business—and it begins by creating enjoyable *employee* experiences. Enjoyment is not the icing on the cake; it allows organizations to take the cake!

REMARK-ABILITY

For customers, remark-ability meant a buying or service experience that was unique, one that created a feeling of "wow!" Employees, meanwhile, want to work for remarkable organizations. They want to work for an organization that cares enough about their input, interests, and feelings that they feel they have a role of significance. Remark-ability is perhaps the most important ability, because it is the sum of what happens when you execute all the other abilities. When you create "wow!" experiences, you not only stimulate customer loyalty; you also create employee pride.

When companies go through downsizing, they often lose that sense of achievement—the remark-ability—that is so desperately needed, especially during times of restructuring. The Academy of Management publication *Executive* recently cited a Louis Harris and Associates study of 406 downsizing companies. The research stated that one out of every five corporations revealed they were losing the "wrong people." In other words, important professionals with vital skills and talents quit their jobs *voluntarily* following a restructuring. Many of those most qualified to revive a moribund organization instead chose other, more attractive career alternatives. If you do not have a remarkable organization, you won't develop that sense of "wow!" and loyalty that accompanies the UEE when you need it most.

Developing a remarkable organization depends on one of the main aspects of show business—creativity. You will become a remarkable organization, one that employees want to work for, by being an innovative organization. You do not become remarkable by putting more into the 401K plan (although that probably wouldn't hurt) but by doing something different and unique. One way to be creative is to use one of the ideas we discussed earlier—*be derivative*.

One of the most remarkable organizations I have ever visited—and one that would be a great model for you to emulate—is found near Muncie, Indiana. In a four-building campus spread over several acres, about sixty people work for a pioneering company that has a global impact—from a restaurant in Kuala Lumpur, Malaysia, to a licensing agreement with an egg company in Argentina, not to mention daily appearances in about 2,600 newspapers worldwide. This organization is the international headquarters of the empire built by local boy-made-good Jim Davis—Paws, Inc.—whose main product is the cartoon cat he created: Garfield.

When you go to meet Jim, you are escorted into a conference room where you are surrounded by Emmys and numerous other awards garnered by the licensed products generated by Paws. The meeting begins and you notice a wonderful aroma—cookies! Hot cookies and milk are served, and immediately the conference becomes a relaxed conversation among friends. (Maybe Jim read the Pepperidge Farm study.)

The remarkable creativity and humility of the leader is contagious. Staff members are obviously having a great time working at Paws—and they don't hesitate to tell you so. Davis entrusts a great deal of responsibility to his colleagues; in fact, he no longer even draws the comic strip. He takes one week to write a month's worth of Garfield installments, then spends the rest of his time leading the multimillion dollar company that deals in licensing, publishing, merchandising, and animation.

Keeping in mind that Garfield is not only a cat but a conglomerate, Davis has innovative ideas to make Paws a remarkable place for his employees to work. The office cafeteria has first-class cuisine. A corporate gymnasium also allows employees the chance to work off the calories. Employees receive points for working out and sticking to a healthy diet. A Paws associate can trade in his or her "healthy points" for a discount in the cafeteria. Paws is supportive of employee efforts for personal development and encourages employee involvement in community activities. In addition, Paws is environmentally conscious; they make recycling and other earth-friendly efforts an integral part of their everyday corporate activities.

Paws is remarkable—in great part because Jim Davis is amazing. But, what employee wouldn't want to work for a company that encouraged good health and fitness, that involved every person in protecting the environment, that rewarded exceptional performance, that fostered a family atmosphere, and that was just an all-around cool place to work? By the way, employee loyalty at Paws borders on religious fervor.

It is easy to dismiss what happens on farmland near Muncie as irrelevant to the situations that most organizations face. You can claim, "But that's show business! It's not my business!"

Really? What prevents you from serving cookies? What is stopping you from initiating measures that cultivate community contributions and family get-togethers? If you fail to provide this Ultimate

Employee Experience to your employees, why should they be loyal to your organization? How will you compete with organizations that are willing to make the commitment to their people to create these kinds of relationships?

Paws may be about entertainment—but it is the prototype organization of the twenty-first century. Because, you see, "ALL Business Is Show Business."

ALL BUSINESS IS SHOW BUSINESS QUIZ

First, make a list of sample high concept statements that could be created by your employees. Then answer the following questions:

- How well do you communicate with your people? Do you *really* listen?

- How well do you establish a team concept within the framework of your organization? Do you provide opportunities for professional gratification and social interaction?

- Write a list of the promises you are making to your employees through your company story. How reliable are you as an organization? Is your word your bond? Is your track record one of consistent performance?

- How customizable are your employees' opportunities? Do you make certain that you make the necessary adjustments in any job to best fit the particular skills of individual employees or groups?

- Is employment with you upgradeable or disposable? Are those in upgradeable positions clearly aware of opportunities for growth and advancement?

- Are you doing a good job of taking care of people in disposable positions so that they will have a positive impact on your customers?

- How much fun is it to work with you? Is enjoyment woven into the fabric of your organization?

- Is your business a remarkable place to work? What remarkable things can you do to create a remarkable experience for your workforce?

EIGHT

THE OBSIDIAN ENTERPRISES STORY

As I sat in the leather chair in the well-appointed Arthur Hills Conference Room at the Hawthorn Country Club near Indianapolis, many words were going through my mind: *Surreal. Dreamlike. Amazing. Extraordinary.* It was almost an out-of-body experience.

My mind went back to the time just a few years earlier when Tim Durham, then living in a one-bedroom apartment, told me how much he liked the principles of "ALL Business Is Show Business." It was at this time that he first brought up the idea of purchasing companies and combining his manufacturing and financial expertise with my business philosophies to enhance their value.

From the first purchase—Lake City Forge—to the most recent, there was great risk and great reward. Yet in each case, the ideas Tim had developed and the philosophy we employed had succeeded. Certainly, we had encountered bumps along the road with every deal and every company. However, we had proven to ourselves and to our partners that this approach was not only visionary but also very profitable.

I shifted in my comfortable chair and brought my attention back to the matter at hand. Tim was standing at the front of the table reviewing the agenda for our meeting. I looked at my friend for the last quarter century and was filled with pride. I felt like the big brother of someone who had just made the winning shot or hit the home run to win the World Series. Tim had done it. He was Chairman and Chief Executive Officer of a profitable, publicly traded company. I was proud to have a role in his production.

I looked down the table at friends like Terry Whitesell, who had worked in lockstep with Tim back in the dark days on the doomed school bus project. Terry is not only the president of Obsidian Enterprises; he's our corporate "sage." He's the wise and experienced executive any organization needs to prevent overly zealous hotshots from sprinting too quickly down the wrong path. On the other hand, Terry is as excited about opportunity and change as any new MBA graduate.

Across the table sat one of my new friends, Jeff Osler, the executive vice president and secretary/treasurer of the company. Jeff had faced the daunting task of learning several new businesses, each unfamiliar to him, in a very short time. He brought both financial acumen and terrific people skills to the position and had made much of the growth that we were experiencing possible.

Then I looked down at the portfolio in front of me on the conference table. It said, "Board of Directors meeting. Obsidian Enterprises, Inc." We were a profitable group of companies. We were now a publicly traded corporation. It was the first official meeting of the Obsidian Board. The dream had come true.

I know that *your* organization can implement the strategies and philosophy of "ALL Business Is Show Business" because *ours* did. Our devotion to this approach was unwavering. As with any management method, however, it is not only the plan but the commitment and the people to implement the plan that makes all the difference. I raise this point for the same reason that automotive manufacturers tell you that your mileage may vary. A half-hearted approach at this

> # The "ALL Business Is Show Business" approach can work for your organization—no matter its size, product, or service—the way it has worked for Obsidian Enterprises.

will bring only moderate results. As I mentioned at the beginning of this book, however, the "ALL Business Is Show Business" approach isn't reserved for organizations in the entertainment industry or high-tech enterprises or large conglomerates. It can work for your organization—no matter its size, product, or service—the way it has worked for Obsidian Enterprises.

Obsidian Enterprises is a highly-disciplined holding company based in Indianapolis that actively purchases and sells companies on a nationwide basis in varied industries. Our stable of companies is constantly changing; however, as of this writing, we currently have a base of six divisions:

1. Pyramid Coach, Inc.—a leading provider of corporate and celebrity entertainer luxury coaches and corresponding equipment

2. Champion Trailer, Inc.—a manufacturer of high-end racing transporters and exhibit trailers

3. United Expressline, Inc.—a manufacturer of steel-framed cargo, racing ATVs, and specialty trailers

4. U.S. Rubber Reclaiming, Inc.—a butyl-rubber reclaiming operation

5. Danzer Industries, Inc.—a manufacturer of service and utility truck bodies and accessories

6. Southwest Expressline—another manufacturer of cargo, racing, and specialty trailers

Before any of our acquisitions, we developed our high concept and powerful story at Obsidian Enterprises. We first created a high concept for our organization: "Creating remarkable value by turning successful organizations into amazing companies." We then built on our high concept at Obsidian by using the power of story, a story that centers around these points: As a company we model our management and marketing upon the philosophy of "ALL Business Is Show Business." We truly believe the purpose of our business is to "create emotional connections that are so satisfying to customers and employees that loyalty is assured." We have reviewed all the companies we believe are executing this strategy and asked ourselves how we can emulate their strengths— and improve on them—for our specific companies. The other aspect to the story is the personal attributes that Tim Durham, Terry Whitesell, Jeff Osler, and myself bring to the table for our investors.

We want to buy undervalued companies that produce quality products that are profitable. We don't believe in turnarounds—or, at least, we don't want one of our own. Our unique spin on this is to buy smaller, profitable companies that are below the radar screen of most mergers and acquisition (M & A) players. We then blend these companies into our existing structure, making all entities more valuable.

We have three additional rules about the companies we consider for purchase:

1. No retail companies

   2. No high-tech companies

   3. No restaurants

Why? Well, we feel the risk in these areas exceeds the reasonable rewards. Many professionals know these types of companies infinitely better than we do. Let them do it. We are different.

To fund the purchases, we have modeled ourselves after KKR (Kohlberg Kravis Roberts), the well-known leveraged buyout kings. Even though we are obviously on a much smaller playing field, buyout firms such as KKR Company follow a basic blueprint. They purchase companies where they can finance the transaction by getting investors to see the likelihood of enhancing their capital investment through: superior management, buying and selling assets, expense reduction, or a combination of all three.

After twenty years of presenting seminars to corporate audiences and reading literally thousands of business books, I understand that any author, speaker, or so-called "business guru" can easily tell you how you should manage your organization, department, or team. (Usually it is not their company—or their money—they are practicing with.) However, I want to show you how Obsidian Enterprises turned the philosophy into the steps we implemented on our road to success.

PYRAMID COACH

Let's examine the case history of one of our companies, Pyramid Coach, the Nashville-based company that provides celebrity coaches primarily to entertainers for transportation to concerts and special events. I'll show you how we integrated our approach into this acquisition.

Pyramid Coach was a fairly successful company we believed to have great potential for enhanced profitability. The previous owners

> **If the "ALL Business Is Show Business" philosophy is not in place right now, that means your organization's value will grow when you implement this approach.**

had done a terrific job of starting the company. They had chosen a great team of managers, drivers, mechanics, and support staff and had built a solid foundation for a successful organization. We also judged that the business model being employed at Pyramid had taken the company about as far as it could go.

At Obsidian, we believe your business model is merely a parallel of your high concept and powerful story. If you haven't defined a high concept and created a story, then you haven't really defined how you are going to do business in a manner that distinguishes you from the competition. If nothing truly separates you from your competitors, then the main point where you are going to have to differentiate yourself is price. This was one of the main challenges Pyramid Coach was facing. They were having a problem of sustaining margins because they were constantly being hammered on the leasing price of their coaches. Don't get me wrong; they were doing a fine job, but there was nothing to separate a Pyramid Coach from the rest of the pack of competitors.

Here's an important point: Since we have distinguished ourselves from other companies with our high concept and story, we do not acquire companies that have already done the same thing. The reason is that if we can find companies that have been moderately successful without this approach, we know we can make them an amazing company by injecting this philosophy into their organization.

Our success means something vital to you: You can enhance your department, organization, or company by doing the same thing. If the "ALL Business Is Show Business" philosophy is not in place right now, that means your organization's value will grow when you implement this approach.

PYRAMID'S HIGH CONCEPT

We developed a high concept when we pursued the financing for Pyramid that we continue to use in the business: "You sing—we'll drive." Notice this high concept tells the artist (Pyramid Coach's client) that he or she doesn't have to worry about anything other than his or her on-stage performance. (Relax, and we will take care of everything else.) Remember the old Greyhound Bus Lines high concept: "Leave the driving to us"? What we wanted was our own unique version of that powerful high concept to address our highly specialized clientele.

Organizing and producing a concert tour is amazingly difficult. From coordination with local promoters and venues to the highly technical aspects of lights and sound, artists and their managers have a large number of issues to worry about every night on the road. We did not want transportation of the tour to be one of their concerns. The more they know that we will handle one of their chief problems—and do so in style—the greater the likelihood we will create a powerful emotional connection that breeds loyalty.

Another thing we want the high concept to accomplish, however, is to get the artist (or his or her management) to start asking questions that would provide an opening for us to tell our powerful story. Remember, as we discussed earlier, the high concept is the foundation for the story. By stating, "You sing—we'll drive," we wanted our prospects to ask, "Well, isn't that what every coach company does?" Our answer to that question is, "No!"—which, naturally, leads into our story and provides a significant point of differentiation.

PYRAMID'S STORY

Next, we developed the powerful story of Pyramid Coach. Much of our story you have already discovered in a previous chapter—Tim Durham's experience as a CEO of a school bus company and the lessons learned from the one bedroom apartment. We told our clients, prospects, employees, and potential investors that what Tim had discovered running a school bus company—and the mistakes that had been made in that process—would help ensure that we knew the potential pitfalls in a celebrity custom bus company. In addition, we emphasized that, unlike some of our competitors, Pyramid was a part of a bigger company—Obsidian—and that meant we could be in the business of providing the best. We were not going to be occasionally strapped for cash as many smaller operations are from time to time. You wouldn't have to worry that we were going to scrimp on maintaining our equipment. (You sing—we'll drive. Remember?)

Then, we enhanced the story—and differentiated ourselves from the former owners of Pyramid—by creating an elite division within our product line called the "Sterling Series." These are coaches with amazing top-line amenities for A-list entertainers. From gold-plated fixtures in the shower to queen-size beds, vanities, marble flooring, lots of mirrors, and top-grade lighting, this is the highest quality transportation in the world. Entertainers are very particular when it comes to the sound systems, and the Sterling Series coaches have Sony flat-screen digital entertainment systems with Datron satellite tracking systems and surround sound, plus VHS and DVD machines, CD changers, and DAT tape machines. Each bunk has flip-down flat screen TVs, all with independent programming that allows our clients on the Sterling Series coaches to watch any program from any source on board to pass the time as they travel down the road. We hired and trained topnotch drivers who would interact well with our unique passengers. We even made the maintenance of the coaches a differentiating point—and a part of our story. Unique to our industry, Pyramid has an on-site maintenance and repair facility. And, in the unlikely event a problem arises on the road, Pyramid contracts with a nationwide network of maintenance facilities. We worked at creating the perception in Nashville that if you had really "made it"—or if you were going to—you needed to be riding in a Pyramid Coach.

We realized we could follow the model of Mercedes and BMW with their product lines. BMW, for example, can put you into one of their 300 series cars for a very reasonable price. If they create the kind of customer experience they should, a relationship is built that will create loyalty—and the purchases of the more expensive 500 and 700 series cars by the same customer in the future. We wanted the Sterling Series to be our flagship, something not everyone could afford, but to which all would aspire. By creating that elite line, we created differentiation for our company from our competition, and from the previous ownership.

Everything was geared toward building on the high concept to create a powerful story that would clearly show that Pyramid is different. We worked very hard to establish the perception that we were the "cream of the crop," the "hip" coach company, *the* place to be. We achieved this by doing everything from taking managers to dinner, to showing up at concerts and meeting the stars, to buying ads in the programs at the Country Music Association and the Academy of Country Music awards programs.

For Tim and me, the reception we would receive from the recording stars when we attended their concerts was always a little amazing. We wanted to create emotional connections with our clients, and one of the best ways you can do that is to simply show up and be interested in their careers. However, they often ended up treating us as if we were the celebrities! As Tim and I discussed it, we realized that from the stars' perspective, they had met hundreds of other entertainers, but we were the first owners of a celebrity coach company they had ever met. Their attitude was a great reinforcement for us, letting us know we were on the right track. Our bus company isn't about buses—it's about relationships.

We were very fortunate when one of our first clients, Brad Paisley, became one of the hottest acts in country music. If you are not familiar with country music, Brad Paisley's career is growing to the point where he will soon be on the level of Garth Brooks or Reba McIntyre. He's the total package as an entertainer—handsome, creative, charismatic, and talented. To me, however, the most impressive thing about Brad is that he is a consummate businessperson. If Brad weren't a singer-songwriter, someday he would be running a Fortune 500 company. Brad bought into our story and became an enthusiastic and loyal client, who is emotionally connected to Pyramid.

Picture a concert venue with several country acts booked to perform. Naturally, the entertainers check out the buses of the other acts, and when Brad would roll in, riding his new Pyramid Coach, he would attract a great deal of attention. The cool thing for us is that Brad would tell these other country music acts how Pyramid was the "hippest" thing happening. When these acts returned from their weekend "gigs," our phones would start ringing.

The power of story really works, especially when you get your clients to become the storytellers! Notice, however, that you have to have your company's story so perfectly designed that it is easy for your clients to repeat to their friends. If we had not followed the rules from the chapter on the power of story, our results would not have been nearly so dramatic.

PYRAMID'S UCE AND UEE

All of us, especially Jennifer George, who handles the day-to-day operations for Pyramid at our base near Nashville, got involved in designing the UCE for our celebrity clients.

One of the challenges that we have faced at Obsidian—and that you may face as you implement this strategy—is the common response: "We've never done it that way around here." To change how a business, department, or organization approaches customers and employees is inherently threatening to some managers. Change implies that the previous way of running the business was wrong. So we take great pains to let managers know they now have the opportunity to enhance their abilities and skills. They also have a greater opportunity to participate in the success and growth of the company, particularly through stock ownership. And they now have the chance to experience greater job satisfaction because they will be creating more fulfilling relationships with customers and colleagues.

Jennifer was already handling the daily activities of Pyramid prior to our takeover. I think she would admit she was a little concerned, at first, about this crazy group who came in with no previous experience in the celebrity coach business. However, she was open to our approaches—and she is now extremely excited about her future and Pyramid's! When Jennifer started seeing results, she realized we were really on to something. Jennifer was the one who helped us realize the important linkage between the Ultimate Employee Experience and the Ultimate Customer Experience. Through the development of a UEE we have reaped some of our biggest dividends—and created an amazing UCE for our clients.

At many entertainment coach companies, the schedules for the drivers are determined much the same way truck drivers are assigned their trips. Usually, a "dispatcher" makes the designations and then dispatches the individual drivers on their "runs" based on the information contained on three lists: the trips that need to be made; the buses that are available to make a run; and the drivers that are available to make trips. Using this information, the dispatcher pairs a driver with a bus, and the trip begins.

That sounds like an efficient way to run the business—but it is a horrible way to create either a UCE or a UEE! When that model is followed, the performer can end up with a different driver for every trip. Since the employee *is* the bus company, this means no emotional connection is established with the bus company. There's no UEE for the driver, either, when the "dispatch" model is followed. Some weeks he could be driving a nice guy like country music's John Michael Montgomery—and next week be taking some acid-rock band of headbangers from show to show. We have a few drivers who would rather transport the heavy metal acts. We try to match them with their preferences.

In addition, under the old, traditional system, one week might find a driver on a brand-new bus, while the next week, he could be steering an old model of another manufacturer down the road. When this happens, the driver feels no pride of ownership in the equipment.

When you provide a UEE to employees, you also make a UCE for your clients much easier to obtain. So we decided to do things differently at Pyramid. Now, we assign a specific bus to a driver. That becomes his or her coach; the drivers are responsible for their buses, and they can even take them home with them and park them there, if that's more convenient. They will be driving the same bus every weekend for as long as they want. Then Jennifer plays matchmaker between the driver and our clients. In this way, we develop emotional connections between the performers and their drivers—and the client knows that he or she is going to be on the same bus every trip, so it becomes a little more like "home" on the road.

You can probably predict what has happened. Prospects first become interested because of our high concept and become hooked because of the power of our story. Once we get them to consider becoming a client, they experience a UCE from a happy employee/driver and from the first-rate equipment. Now, our customer loyalty is off the charts. We find that our artists are out promoting our services to other artists through word-of-mouth referrals, just as Brad Paisley did in our early days. Meanwhile, employees are happy because we provide them a UEE—and they are exceedingly dedicated.

One residual benefit is that our maintenance costs are declining because our approach provides both entertainers and drivers with a high degree of emotional connection—in other words, the pride of ownership. Therefore, they are taking greater care of the bus while it is on the road. The better they treat the coach when they are on the road, the less we have to spend to fix it when they return home.

ALL THE ASPECTS WORK TOGETHER

We have focused on every aspect of the "ALL Business Is Show Business" approach at Pyramid Coach:

- High Concept
- Power of Story
- UCE

- UEE
- The "Abilities" that Customers Want
- The "Abilities" that Employees Want

Through our focus on these steps, combined with a lot of hard work from a very dedicated and inspired team, this division of Obsidian Enterprises has provided amazing returns to our investors by generating significant profits. In fact, the way in which Obsidian grew to become a publicly traded company is another example of the benefits of using the "ALL Business Is Show Business" approach.

DEVELOPING THE OBSIDIAN CAPITAL PARTNERS INVESTMENT FUND

Early in the development of our company, Tim analyzed our situation and quickly came to the conclusion that we would be much better off if we were not only the owners and managers, but if we could also provide our own capital. To do that, we decided to form a fund—a pool of investment capital—to assist the financing of our future acquisitions. This would also allow us to look for bigger and better businesses to bring into our group, benefiting the growth of the new companies, as well as adding efficiencies to our current divisions.

The decision was made that we would go to individuals, rather than solely to bankers or mezzanine investment groups, and ask them to invest in our fund. In other words, we had to convince wealthy individuals they were going to get better returns on their money by investing it in our fund than they would putting it into the stock market or other investment instruments they had chosen. It was a daunting task; in essence, it was telling rich people that we could do better with their money than they were! However, because of our ability to develop a strategic approach that had differentiation from other potential investments, combined with our successful track record, we were able to create a business plan that connected exceedingly well with potential investors.

I don't mean to oversimplify the process here. This was *very* hard work. However, by realizing that "ALL Business Is Show Business," and having the high concept and story I related earlier, we distinguished ourselves throughout the process from others seeking investment capital. Because they were distinct and compelling, our business plans and proposals stood out to potential investors. That is, to a great degree, why they were successful. (If you cannot create a presentation that is emotionally compelling and amazing—why in the world should any investor believe you can create an exciting, vibrant, and successful company?)

Our success in raising capital through the fund allowed us to make several purchases, including Pyramid Coach.

GOING PUBLIC

One of Tim Durham's goals was to be the chairman and major shareholder of a publicly traded company. Now, with the strength of Obsidian, it was time, once again, to change the structure of our business. Tim's idea was to model Warren Buffett's approach. As you may be aware, Buffett privately owned several businesses before he purchased the publicly traded Berkshire Hathaway. He then rolled the companies he owned into Berkshire, making them all available on the public market. Tim wanted us to do the same.

By becoming a public company, we would be able to use our own stock to make future purchases and have the capital available from the public markets to reinvest in our current businesses, if needed. In addition, according to Tim Durham's analysis, the growth of a publicly traded company yields a better reward through the stock market—

because of the corresponding increase in share price and market capitalization—than the growth of a private company through its preceived valuation and potential sales price.

Another important factor to all of us was that, as a public company, we could make available an Employee Stock Ownership Plan to our dedicated employees, allowing them to share in our growth and development. It was another step in providing them with a UEE. Every financial step was taken for one crucial reason: to enhance our opportunities to profitably create emotional connections with customers and employees to ensure their loyalty.

Now came the task of finding the right company. As Jeff Osler said, "One of our toughest jobs is figuring out which company makes the most sense for us to acquire. We'll search through one thousand or more opportunities to find just the right one." In other words, just like in show business, what goes on behind the scenes is difficult and sometimes grueling. It pays off, however, when the performance begins. Then, the second hardest part begins: ascertaining the right price to pay for the business.

"You've got to realize," Osler explained, "that emotion is the dominant factor in all of this—not money. The owners, in most cases, have a great amount of emotion wrapped up in their companies. We have to convince them that we are the right people to carry on their work—yet, at the same time, get the best price we can. In addition, because they are so much 'in love' with their companies, it is often difficult for them to establish a price for their business that makes strong economic sense for us.

"One of our secrets to success," he continued, "is that we get the emotions and perceptions in the right place first. That enables us to deal with the economic steps in a positive and productive manner. It *is* show business."

After searching through many opportunities, we selected Danzer

Industries of Hagerstown, Maryland. Danzer is the manufacturer of Danzer-Morrison brand (as well as private label) utility and service truck bodies that are sold to the truck equipment industry. Sales are handled through both a distribution network and directly to national accounts. The company has a long and successful history since its beginning in 1886 as a sheet metal works firm. Over its history, Danzer built a variety of products before evolving its focal point into the truck bodies and accessories it now manufactures.

Danzer Industries had earlier purchased Morrison, Incorporated, a large truck body manufacturer. At that point, the company began developing the Danzer-Morrison label. The current product line, manufactured in the 75,000-square-foot factory, includes standard service, high roof, cab over, crane, aerial lift, and platform truck bodies. It also includes smaller items such as pickup utility toppers, backpacks, and toolboxes. The facility is equipped with state-of-the-art metal forming and fabricating equipment.

After a short negotiation, a deal was consummated. In a complex financial transaction, Obsidian Enterprises—now renamed "Obsidian Enterprises, Incorporated" to reflect that we are much more than a financial company—became a public company. Our common stock of Obsidian Enterprises currently trades on the NASDAQ OTC Bulletin Board under the symbol "OBSD."

THE FUTURE

As Terry Whitesell said, "We have to constantly be vigilant about our businesses. Many times companies will get excited about something new—perhaps even use the 'show-business' approach on them—and forget that they must continue to use that philosophy on the businesses they already have."

He continued, "We have to try to anticipate where each of our existing companies should be three, five, and ten years from now. In addition, we need to examine what companies we could add to our line that fit our present situation, or move us into different segments where we need to be."

Whitesell also stated, "It is not easy—and it never will be. We're not a company that is sitting on a pile of cash, and changes in the economy and the market make it difficult. However, we have established strong bonds with our customers, employees, and suppliers. We're well positioned for continued growth and profitability."

Jeff Osler added, "Our commitment to the show-business approach and building emotional connections has also impacted and improved our ability to communicate with one another. A truck body manufacturer might not think they have anything to share with a company that makes drag racing trailers—but they do. Perhaps they have a manufacturing or engineering idea—or they might be scheduling a shipment of parts that can be shared with another one of our divisions, thereby saving expenses for both. The only way we can make certain these folks are talking and sharing with one another is when they are emotionally connected as a part of the Obsidian team."

Tim Durham revealed what he predicts for the future of Obsidian (and provided great advice for all managers) when he said, "I think the two keys are perseverance and impatience."

He added, "I know that the two may sound contradictory, but they are not. We built this company by being both—and this company will grow the same way. Perseverance is not giving up until the deal is done. Most professionals give up when someone, or two or three someones, say 'no.' At Obsidian, once we set a target, we do not give up until the deal is done."

Tim continued, "Impatience means you are willing to force the issue to get things done. We have an eagerness, a keenness to make things happen. Perhaps one of our biggest attributes is that we really do believe that 'ALL Business Is Show Business.' We must build emotional connections with clients and employees and create a positive perception about what we do in the marketplace."

Tim asked, "Why is Microsoft worth about $62 a share today, when it was worth about twice as much in January 2000? Is Microsoft's true value less?"

Then came Tim's important answer to his own question: "Absolutely not. There's no way that Microsoft is half the company it was a couple of years ago. The difference is that the *perception* of Microsoft's value has changed. Markets do not change based upon value—it is the public's perception of value that sets the share price.

"That's why all of this work on creating emotional connections is so important. Loyal customers and employees are not only great for every organization—they also help you establish the kind of perception in the marketplace that companies crave. And what industry is better at creating and managing public perceptions than the entertainment business? All of us can—and should—learn from their expertise," Durham concluded.

WHAT'S IN A NAME

The Merriam-Webster Collegiate Dictionary defines obsidian as "a dark natural glass formed by the cooling of molten lava." According to the website MineralGalleries.com, "Obsidian is the result of volcanic lava coming in contact with water. Often the lava pours into a lake or ocean and is cooled quickly. This process produces a glassy texture in the resulting rock. Obsidian has been used by ancient people as a cutting tool, for weapons, and for ceremonial purposes."

Many times in business, there is a lot of sound and fury—just like the volcanic eruption that produces the molten lava—with nothing of real value left behind. We love the word "obsidian," because our goal is to be different, to be like the obsidian stone. With our company, after the fire and heat of the manufacturing process, we want that which remains to be useful and meaningful and, in its own way, a thing of beauty.

The manufacturing process creates products—but people create relationships. When you create emotional connections, you have formed something functional (similar to the manner in which ancient people used obsidian). However, you have also created something of value (as obsidian is used today) that can stand the test of time.

That's the goal for our organization. I hope it is for yours, as well. Then, you, too, can say what I said to myself that morning at our first Board of Directors meeting: The dream has come true.

ALL BUSINESS IS SHOW BUSINESS QUIZ

- What does your story have in common with Obsidian's?

- List the qualities found in Obsidian you would like your organization to model. What practical steps can you take to ensure that your organization utilizes these qualities in its day-to-day functioning?

NINE

AS THE CURTAIN RISES

The points I have been making throughout this book were driven home to me recently by a stockbroker in Manhattan. We were chatting about the challenges she had been facing in her business because of the volatility in the stock market, combined with the economic impact of the tragedies of September 11, 2001. She refused to let the events that were happening dictate to her the level of professional success she was going to attain.

BEYOND PRODUCT

"When I went through my training to become a broker," she told me, "just about everything we learned was about the products we would be selling to our clients. Mutual funds, stocks, bonds, annuities, and so forth. I wasn't having much success getting my career off the ground, so I went to a sales training program. There I learned many techniques to close a sale—features and benefits, rapport building, forty ways to secure agreement—stuff like that. Frankly, it didn't improve my business all that much. Then I realized that anyone could learn those tricks. And everyone has product. What no one else could duplicate was *me*! Every time I talked to a client or prospect, I was on stage for them. My passion, my commitment, the experiences I could create for clients and prospects—I realized I had a monopoly in the marketplace on that!"

When the stockbroker in Manhattan said those words, a powerful simplicity in her phrases struck me. From computers to cars, from furniture stores to flower shops, from General Electric to a general store, everybody has product. Yet, as she so eloquently implied, it is what you do *beyond* product that makes all the difference in business.

Please do not misunderstand what I am trying to say; having a superior product is incredibly important and powerful. Yet no customer is loyal to a product. Customers become loyal to the *experience* that is created by the mixture of the product with the service, feelings, benefits, and advantages they encounter as a result of their use of the product.

Managers often make mistakes because, like the Manhattan stockbroker, they do not connect what they have been taught and trained to do with what the changing marketplace desires. Several basic errors contribute to our inability to create compelling experiences for our customers and our employees. Here are three in particular:

1. Working harder at the old plan

2. Placing economic connections before emotional connections

3. Believing that "price is king"

WORKING HARDER AT THE OLD PLAN

The "work ethic" is a great thing. However, never before have we seen people working so hard and so long with so many tools to accomplish so little. If your current strategy—which may have worked beautifully just a short time ago—isn't creating the results needed in today's market, why work harder at the old plan?

When production goals aren't achieved, the natural assumption that most managers make is that we have to "bear down and work harder." The whip is cracked and often there is hell to pay. I've seen many sales managers tell their salespeople that they aren't "making enough calls." Of course, that's the old plan; more calls mean more sales, right?

As we now know, the answer is, "Not necessarily."

A company that is a client of mine has two divisions that each have a product sold through the same distributor network. In other words, both Division A's product and Division B's product are retailed through the independent offices of another company; we'll call it the XYZ company.

Division A assigned a large number of salespeople to small territories who would frequently visit XYZ. They would take a very aggressive selling approach and focus totally on the product. Division A constantly demanded more and more calls from their salespeople. The philosophy was "burn and churn"; if some salespeople couldn't stand the pace, they would leave and be replaced. Product was the king, not the people.

Division B took the show-business approach, building emotional relationships. They employed a much smaller team of professionals, but Division B made a strong commitment to their people and set up compensation plans that encouraged them to develop partnerships to help develop the business of the XYZ Company. They started a speaker's bureau and provided the services of consultants and experts to assist the professionals of XYZ in building their profitability. In turn, emotional connections were created between XYZ and Division B that fostered loyal relationships. Because of the relationships and emotional links, XYZ felt very comfortable selling the product of Division B.

Division B is selling millions of their products; Division A is still trying to gain access to the real decision makers at XYZ. And perhaps most important, soon the divisions will be merged, with the manager of B having total responsibility. The president of the parent company wants the show-business approach implemented throughout the organization. The manager of Division A recently said he just "wished the market was better and his people had worked harder." He still doesn't get it.

Don't just "*think* outside the box"; *plan* and *do* outside the box!

PLACING ECONOMIC CONNECTIONS BEFORE EMOTIONAL CONNECTIONS

Obviously, if your organization doesn't succeed economically, it has no viability. However, many managers fail to understand that emotional connections precede economic ones. If you get the emotional connections in place properly, the economic associations will follow. Even those companies that advertise that they are the "low price leaders" within their respective industries—Wal-Mart and Southwest Airlines, for example—still have to create positive feelings about doing business with them before customers will sample their low prices.

Businesses are constantly evaluating how they are doing from an economic standpoint—and they clearly should. Many companies, however, spend *no* time judging how they are fulfilling customer and employee needs from an emotional standpoint. That has to change. The problem in business seems akin to that in medicine. Future doctors spend an enormous time in medical school learning the technical skills of their profession. And don't get me wrong—that's a great thing! I want the doctors who treat my family and me to have a superior amount of technical skill. However, they receive little training in the aspect that will be one of the most important of their medical careers—managing their personal, emotional relationships with patients.

Whether we acquire our business acumen through university

courses, in-house corporate training, practical experience, or a combination of all three, precious little time is spent on the aspect that will
allow us to differentiate our organizations and ourselves—managing
our personal, emotional relationships with clients and colleagues.
Remember the old cliché: Before they care how much you know, they
have to know how much you care.

BELIEVING THAT "PRICE IS KING"

Price matters. There's no doubt about it. Naturally, I want to pay a
competitive price for anything and everything I purchase. I want to
make a good deal and I don't want to think I have paid more for
something than someone else who has chosen the exact same thing.
That's a normal and natural part of consumer behavior.

Still, price isn't all that matters, no matter what some think. Take
drinking water as an example. Water is free at water fountains in every
public building and park. Just go to your tap and turn it on. Did that
stop Evian or Perrier? Did they say, "Well, who would pay for water?"
Absolutely not! They created a unique perception about their product.
By the same token, did Starbucks say, "Wait—you can get coffee just
about anywhere? Why would people go out of their way to get it from
us? We'd better be the cheapest or else they won't make the effort!"
Just the opposite! In fact, you could argue that in the case of Starbucks,
high price is a differentiating factor; it's part of the aura of their success. So if other organizations can make coffee and drinking water into
products for which customers are willing to pay a premium, what
excuse do you have that you can't do the same with your products and
services?

Many of the challenges we face when it comes to pricing stem
from our inability to creatively develop strategies that differentiate
our products and services in a manner that provides a compelling

emotional experience to the customer. As we discussed many times in this book, customers crave differentiation. If you don't create uniqueness for the customer, they'll provide their own in the easiest way they know how: by asking for a cheaper price. However, when you realize you are "on stage"—that ALL business *is* show business—you can create such a compelling emotional connection that you can make *anything* (even water and coffee) a highly unique experience.

In this chapter, let me share with you a few suggestions that will help you better accomplish this goal.

DETERMINE YOUR BUSINESS

When beginning a seminar I will often ask professionals to answer this simple question: "What business are you in?" Naturally, most will answer with a pretty standard, and specific, definition. "I'm in the car business," for example. My response is to say that the "car business" is your industry, not your business. When you understand what business you are involved in, you hopefully avoid the errors we've just discussed. Here are the businesses in which all of us are involved.

THE EMOTION BUSINESS

You have specialists who manage the financial and economic aspects of your organization, yet you probably haven't given too much thought to the management of the emotional aspects of your company. How your customers and employees *feel* about you, your department, your organization, and your business will be much more important than the facts about what you do.

When the airlines were cutting employees by the thousands after the terrorist attack of September 2001, local television stations in Los Angeles broadcast a story about some American Airlines employees who had worked for the airline for two decades; according to the story as it was reported, they were fired by E-mail from the corporate headquarters. The employees—who were also told to continue to work at local ticketing offices in the L.A. area for a few additional days—were shown on camera weeping as they were helping customers.

Even if you give American the benefit of the doubt that the cost-cutting measure was economically necessary, wasn't there a better emotional way to handle the situation? What kind of feelings did this action create among other employees? The action was so troubling that, if the report is accurate, it makes me less likely to fly American again. If, after more than twenty years of service, an employee cannot be treated with dignity, what does that say for the treatment a customer will receive? How can the airlines expect their employees to be of service to customers and encourage loyalty, when they know they can't count on it from their employer?

Apparently, no one thought about that. Companies are going to have to learn that they can make decisions that are economically correct—but if they implement them in a manner that is emotionally bankrupt, they will pay a steep financial price.

You are in the emotion business. The way you obtain loyalty from customers and employees is, in part, through the strategic creation of positive emotional experiences.

THE PERCEPTION BUSINESS

We have heard experts on communication say that "perception is reality." However, we have often failed to understand that principle when it comes to business. Tim Durham's example from the previous chapter about the stock price of Microsoft is a perfect illustration. Perception drives the stock market. And perception motivates the kind of loyalty we want to acquire from customers and employees.

For many years, I flew a large number of miles on Northwest Airlines. After an incredibly bad service experience, I stopped giving Northwest my business. I know it tracks my frequent flyer miles, because I get periodic statements in the mail. Couldn't Northwest easily have had some kind of "red flag" on accounts that showed a dramatic drop in business? Yet, after years of loyalty, I never received a note from the airline asking, "Where did you go? What can we do to get your business back?" As a result, my perception was that it obviously didn't care too much about my business—or else it would have wondered where it went! However, if it had inquired, my perception would have been totally different; I would have felt like somebody noticed. That would have made a giant impression.

Are you tracking your customers' loyalty? Are you creating the right perceptions about how much you care?

I do a lot of work with a company that has a new CEO. He has a plan for turning the company around, a plan that makes great economic sense. However, he is perceived by most in the organization to be someone who doesn't care about the people who work for him. There-fore, he will get neither the productivity nor the commitment from the very people who are essential in the execution of his plans. I do not believe his company is going to make it. I also believe the reason it will not isn't because of his economic strategy, but rather because his colleagues' perception of him is so bad that few want to be on his team.

People won't get on board with you if they perceive you can't get them where they want to go. However, you will be amazed by what they will do if they perceive you can deliver what they want. Revolutionary products are created by leaders who, like Steve Jobs, for example, can inspire the perception that people are a part of something "insanely great."

SHOW BUSINESS

I'll say it one more time: whatever your product or service, in today's world you must realize that your business isn't just about what you do—it is about the performance you give when you are "on stage" before customers and employees and how that serves to create experiences they want to repeat.

During the economic downturn experienced at the onset of the 21st century, the food service business reported a dramatic rise in customers for those restaurants that served "comfort food"—meat loaf, steak, and potatoes, the old standards. Why? Because restaurants aren't just about food; they are about experiences. State Farm Insurance, to use another example, could simply say "Give us money now, and we'll give your spouse a check when you die." Instead, of course, they tell us that they're "like a good neighbor."

The success of this high concept goes well beyond a mere slogan. It means that my State Farm agent realizes he is "on stage" every single time we talk about my insurance needs; he needs to convince me he is a "good neighbor." He needs to deliver a performance that will satisfy not only my financial requirements and plans but also my need for an emotional experience that will make me want to come back and buy more insurance and send my friends to him for their policies.

Any actor realizes that no matter how she feels, or what has happened in her personal life that day, or what kind of mood her fellow cast mates are in, or what the weather is, or how large the particular audience is for that day's show—despite all these factors, each and every performance must be executed with perfection and passion. It is her responsibility to use her training and talent to create an amazing experience for the audience.

I want the managers where I buy my stocks and bonds—and rent cars and go to service my computers and eat and sleep overnight and on and on—to understand the very same thing. I want them to emphasize that fact—and inspire similar perfect, passionate performances—with their employees.

GET A PERFORMING PARTNER

Show business is full of examples of superstars getting their start by working closely with others. From Dean Martin and Jerry Lewis, who worked together as a comedy team before their individual successes, to Mike Myers, Adam Sandler, and other former members of the cast of *Saturday Night Live*, show business knows that creativity and productivity are often enhanced through collaboration.

If you're a young professional, find a mentor. If you happen to be a seasoned professional, locate some young rebel. Share the ideas in this book that have appealed to you and work together to create concepts specific to your organization. Stimulate unique thinking and motivate each other to action. Hold your partner responsible for getting things done—and have him or her do the same with you.

CONTEMPLATION CREATES A BETTER PRESENTATION

I've presented more than two thousand speeches in front of audiences as large as 25,000 people—and yet I am still nervous prior to every single presentation. My mentor in the business, the late Grady Nutt, always used to tell me, "It isn't nervousness—it's 'performance anxiety.' You want to do a good job, so you are anxious. Take some time and get your thoughts together."

Taking some time and getting our thoughts together is a great idea before any performance, no matter the stage. We have all seen performers who have great command when they perform. They fill up the arena in concert; they jump off the TV or movie screen with their charisma. You need to have this kind of control of the situation whenever and wherever you perform. To achieve this power, every entertainer and speaker I know will take just a moment before the performance to "get centered" and become "audience-focused," to get into the mindset necessary for presenting the best performance possible.

Develop a checklist of what's important. Take a quick look prior to every call, staff meeting, or review. This doesn't take a lot of time; it merely takes the discipline to stop for a moment and center your thoughts—and yourself.

When you are passionate about your topic, you can easily get carried away. Some professionals have become so excited about their favorite concepts that they run the risk of turning their colleagues off to their ideas. They need to take a few moments and contemplate before they present their thoughts.

My speech coach Ron Arden of San Diego says, "You should not speak from the heart." That's a shocking statement when we want to be passionate and compelling with our "show biz" communication. But Arden goes on to counsel, "You should write and prepare what you have to say from the heart. You should *speak* from skill."

Develop your communication to employees and clients from your heart and emotions. Then present the communication after contemplation. Focus on your skills.

MAINTAIN "PERFORMANCE SHAPE"

I had the thrill of seeing Elvis Presley in concert during his first tour of the early 1970s. It was an amazing show—Elvis prowled the stage like a panther. He showed off his karate moves and danced and sang without ever losing a beat. He was absolutely mesmerizing.

I will never forget talking with my mother on the phone after she had attended an Elvis concert several years later. By this time, Elvis was overweight, couldn't move without becoming winded, and at one point even lay down on the stage, flat on his back, to sing a song. My mom was crushed. He was no longer the Elvis of her dreams; to her, he was now just an out-of-shape man.

Have you ever seen an action movie that was unintentionally funny because the star was out of shape and obviously couldn't do the stunts he was pretending to do on the screen? Part of creating emotional connections is projecting a sense of congruency. You'll have a harder time convincing clients and colleagues that you are focused if you eat, drink, and smoke too much. What people see speaks more loudly than what you say.

This isn't a "fitness book." And I'm not suggesting that you have to look like Tom Cruise or Halle Berry to be successful in your "show business." Remember, however, you are in the perception business. Fair or not, we presume that fit companies are managed by fit people. As my friend Michael LeBoeuf says, "If you don't invest the time to be healthy, you will have to make the time to be sick."

FOCUS ON SUCCESS AND LEARN FROM FAILURE

During the interviews I conducted with many celebrities during my days as a movie reviewer, I was always impressed how the superstars kept a constant focus on what they really wanted to achieve in their profession. John Travolta told me he read every single script that anyone gave him. Arnold Schwarzenegger started several little businesses before he became famous so that he would have an income stream that meant he didn't have to take insignificant acting jobs just to keep food on the table. We've all heard and read the many other stories of present-day stars who waited tables and worked as carpenters so they could continue to pursue their dreams while dealing with the rejection of failed auditions.

The lesson you can learn from them is to practice a dual focus on the success you want, while learning from the failures you encounter. Keep your high concept in front of you. Repeatedly examine your story. Relentlessly refine your UCE and UEE strategies. Constantly ask yourself this question: "What specific action can I take today that will help me and my organization profitably create experiences that our customers and employees want to repeat?"

And meanwhile, understand that things won't always work out the way you want. That's why we must commit ourselves to making failure our laboratory for future success. Every change we make—especially when it comes to changing our philosophy of business—involves risk. As one prominent advertising campaign is saying, "The greatest risk is not taking one."

When we change, we risk. When we risk, we sometimes fail. However, when we learn from our failures, we pave the road to success. In his book *Failing Forward,* John Maxwell states, "In life, the question is not if you will have problems, but how you are going to deal with them. Stop failing backward and start failing forward!" In part, the way you "fail forward" is to take responsibility and learn from each mistake.

DON'T LET THE CRITICS GRIND YOU DOWN

When the entertainment scene was my responsibility, I always referred to myself as a "movie reviewer" rather than a "movie critic." The difference may seem insignificant, but it had a subtle power for me.

The term "reviewer" implied to me that I was going to go to a movie and then tell my television audience what my impressions were about the film. I was free to get enthusiastic about what I liked—as well as tell my viewers what I found disappointing. I went to every single movie—a minimum of one per week for over ten years—with the hope and expectation that I was going to see something worthwhile.

A "critic," on the other hand, seemed to me to be someone who went to the film with the intention to criticize. He or she would search for what was wrong so they could tell their readers or viewers about the movie's weaknesses. Many of the so-called "critics" I knew played as if it were a blood sport. They loved taking famed directors and actors to task. For some, I suspect that disparaging successful performers made them feel a little more successful and worthwhile themselves.

We see the same phenomenon in business every day, and you will notice it even more as you shape your organization toward the "Show Business" approach. If you let the critics have their way, you will never accomplish the fundamental changes in your organization that today's culture requires.

Sometimes we erroneously presume that critics know what they are talking about. That is not the case. "Can't sing. Can't act. Can dance a little." That was one critic's impression when he saw Fred Astaire for the first time. An executive at ABC in 1984 was highly critical of the pilot episode of a television sitcom and passed on the show because he stated that the program didn't have "bite," and that audiences wouldn't watch "an unrealistic portrayal of blacks." So Bill Cosby took his program to NBC.

In your business, you need to know the difference between the reviewers—who will tell you the good *and* the bad—and the critics, who only want to criticize.

THE "DO" GAP

Relatively few businesses actually *execute* strategies that will enhance their organizations. As I said earlier, we get so busy doing what we do—and so caught up in the office politics, the "cufflinks" I mentioned in a previous chapter—that we do not accomplish nearly as much as we could and should. Back in the 1970s, I heard a speaker talk about the fact that we do not have an information gap in business. He said we have a "*do* gap." We do not lack for information; we are deficient in execution. As business philosopher Jim Rohn once said, "We major in minor things."

To make a difference, the concepts in this book must be *applied*.

Why do we continue to talk about the same business leaders over and over—Bill Gates, Warren Buffett, Jack Welch, Herb Kelleher, and Steve Jobs, for example? Because these individuals rocked the boat. They and their companies provide examples for our changing times. Too often, however, we learn the lesson intellectually and fail to implement it strategically. We fall victim to the "we've never done it that way before" syndrome.

Motivational speaker Anthony Robbins says that "Motion creates emotion." This implies that if you want to create emotional connections with customers and employees, you have to *move*! The challenge is this: *do something!* When I pick up my Bible I find no chapter called "Wishes" or "Hopes" or "Dreams" or "Wants." There is one, however, entitled *"Acts."* Two thousand years ago, just like today, the challenge facing individuals was to *act* on the knowledge they held in their minds and the beliefs they held in their hearts. When they did, they changed the world.

You too can be an "act-or"—*one who takes action.*

Thoreau wrote, "Most men lead lives of quiet desperation;" I believe that many men and women—executives and entrepreneurs, supervisors and staffs—lead careers of quiet complacency. These times call for something different—*something dramatic!* If you don't rock the boat just a little, it will eventually sink.

YOUR CHALLENGE

- **Create a high concept statement** that is short, attention grabbing, powerful, and unique. Develop such an interesting statement that listeners can't help but ask you to tell them more.

- Using the high concept as your foundation, **craft a powerful story** that creates a compelling case for customers and employees to become connected to your organization. Use your history—combined with your vision of the future—as a promise to your customers and employees.

- **Design the Ultimate Customer Experience** (UCE) and the Ultimate Employee Experience (UEE). Deliver upon the promise of your story and engineer the systems necessary to create this experience for every customer, every employee, every time.

- **Develop the systems** necessary to execute the "abilities" that customers and employees really want. Then measure your performances so you can enhance and improve your execution.Because of the power of its message, I conclude all of my speeches with the following poem:

TOMORROW

He would be all that a mortal could be—Tomorrow
No one would be kinder or fairer than she—Tomorrow

Each day he would stack the letters he would write—Tomorrow
She'd think of the clients she'd fill with delight—Tomorrow

But the fact is they died and faded from view
And all that was left when their living was through
Was the mountain of things they intended to do—Tomorrow.

—EDGAR GUEST (adapted)

LET'S KEEP IN TOUCH

I truly believe that the "show business" metaphor strikes at the heart of what *all* businesses need to be doing in these changing times. That is why I issue you an invitation—and a challenge. The invitation is to visit our web site at www.allbizisshowbiz.com. On our web site you will find a community bulletin board where you will be able to post what you have done to make your business a "show business." You will also have the opportunity to read about the accomplishments and challenges of your fellow show business "stars." By sharing ideas with one another—and by warning each other of potential stumbles—we will be able to assist each other in developing the kind of organizations we all want to achieve. I will also provide updates of what managers, entrepreneurs, executives, and all employees are sharing with me as I travel the world presenting programs on the subject.

Here's to rave reviews, constant sequels, and standing ovations from your customers and employees!

If you would like more information on Scott McKain's speeches and seminars, contact your favorite speakers bureau, or:

Barry Jeffrey, Vice President
William Morris Agency
2100 West End Avenue; Suite 100
Nashville, Tennessee 37203
Phone: 615.963.3000
Fax: 615.963.3090

For information about Scott's consulting services, video and audio programs and other projects of assistance to companies seeking to implement the "ALL Business is Show Business" approach, contact:

Ted Greene, Senior Vice-President
Dreamcatcher Artist Management
2908 Poston Avenue
Nashville, Tennessee 37203
Phone: 615.329.2303
Fax: 615.986.3277

For information about Obsidian Enterprises, contact Scott at:

Scott McKain, Vice Chairman
Obsidian Enterprises
111 Monument Circle; Suite 3680
Indianapolis, Indiana 46204

Or, visit our websites:

www.allbizisshowbiz.com
www.scottmckain.com
www.experienceconsultinggroup.com
www.dreamcatcherenter.com